W0289636

Eva Werner

Besser in

Englisch

7. Klasse

Gymnasium

Cornelsen
SCRIPTOR

Über die Autorin:
Eva Werner unterrichtet Englisch an einem Gymnasium.

Bildquellen:
Fotolia/DeVIce, S. 105 oben
picture alliance/dpa, S. 105 unten

Bibliografische Information der Deutschen Nationalbibliothek
Die Deutsche Nationalbibliothek verzeichnet diese Publikation in der Deutschen Nationalbibliografie; detaillierte bibliografische Daten sind im Internet über http://dnb.d-nb.de abrufbar.

2. Auflage

Bibliographisches Institut GmbH
Dudenstraße 6, 68167 Mannheim

Redaktionelle Leitung: Constanze Schöder
Redaktion: lüra - Klemt & Mues GbR
Illustrationen: Dorina Teßmann
Herstellung: Annette Scheerer
Layoutkonzept: Horst Bachmann, Weinheim
Umschlaggestaltung: glas AG, Seeheim-Jugenheim
Satz/Layout: Carola Fuchs, Berlin
Druck und Bindung: orthdruk, Białystok
Printed in Poland

ISBN 978-3-411-87026-4

Liebe Schülerin, lieber Schüler,

du hast hier ein Buch zum Lernen, Wiederholen und Üben in der Hand.

- Die Themen sind in kleinen, verständlichen Schritten aufbereitet.
  Schaffe dir parallel zu diesem Buch ein Arbeitsheft an, in das du hineinschreiben kannst.
- Ein Lösungsheft hilft dir, deine Ergebnisse zu kontrollieren.
- Mit der beiliegenden CD und vielen Übungen dazu kannst du dein Hörverstehen trainieren.
  Folgender Hinweis zeigt dir, wo du die CD verwenden musst: **Track**

Mit diesem Buch kannst du auf zweierlei Weise arbeiten:

1. Möglichkeit:
Wenn du dich im Fach Englisch insgesamt ein wenig unsicher fühlst, solltest du das Buch von vorn bis hinten durcharbeiten. Nimm dir aber nicht zu viel auf einmal vor. Bearbeite lieber kleinere Abschnitte und arbeite dafür regelmäßig, vielleicht sogar täglich.

2. Möglichkeit:
Vielleicht kommst du eigentlich gut zurecht, hast aber einige Lücken? Kläre genau, am besten mithilfe deiner Lehrerin oder deines Lehrers, wo deine Lücken sind. Sieh im Inhaltsverzeichnis nach, wähle einzelne Abschnitte aus und arbeite sie durch.

GOOD TO KNOW **Zum Arbeiten mit diesem Buch**

- Manche Aufgaben kannst du im Buch lösen. Benutze ein **Arbeitsheft,** wenn du viel schreiben musst.
- Bist du beim Lösen der Übungsaufgaben unsicher, schau dir die **Beispiele** dazu noch einmal an.
- Vergleiche deine Ergebnisse immer sorgsam mit dem **Lösungsheft**. Überprüfe genau, was du falsch gemacht hast. Aus Fehlern kann man gut lernen.
- Bearbeite dieselben Aufgaben nach einigen Tagen noch einmal.
  Die **Wiederholung** schafft Sicherheit.

Viel Spaß beim Lernen!

1 Revision

Prüfe, was du schon kannst!

Mit den Übungen in diesem Wiederholungsteil kannst du herausfinden, ob du mit diesem Band arbeiten kannst.

- ▷ Führe die Übungen durch.
- ▷ Für jede richtige Lösung bekommst du einen Punkt. Trage deine Punktzahl ein und zähle sie dann auf Seite 15 zusammen.
- ▷ Vielleicht zeigt dein Ergebnis, dass du besser erst einmal den Stoff von Klasse 6 wiederholen solltest.

1 Put in the verbs. You have to decide: Present or past tense? Simple or progressive?

This morning Peter met his friend Andrew ...

"Hey Andrew, where ________ (you/go)?"

"I ________ (be) on my way home," Andrew ________ (reply).

Peter ________ (ask)," ________ (you/want/hear) what ________ (happen) to me last Saturday?"

"Well," Andrew ________ (say), "OK, I ________ (have) some time left."

They ________ (sit) down on a bench and Peter ________ (tell) his story.

"I ________ (be) in the record shop, when suddenly I ________ (hear) a strange sound and ________ (feel) something cold in my neck. I ________ (be) really scared and ________ (run) out of the shop into a small street. I ________ (not want) to look but I ________ (can not close) my eyes and then I ________ (see) it: a big, terrible ghost!" "Stop it, Peter," Andrew ________ (cry). "You ________ (tell) lies (= Lügen) again!". And he ________ (go) home.

You get 1 point for each correct answer. **Your points:** ________ /21

REMEMBER *Present perfect or simple past?*

Das *present perfect* drückt aus, dass etwas in der Vergangenheit begonnen hat, aber jetzt immer noch andauert, bzw. die Wirkung momentan noch spürbar ist.
Das *simple past* wird für in der Vergangenheit abgeschlossene Dinge verwendet.

2 Present perfect or past tense?

1. Sarah has lost her keys again. It's the second time this ________ (happen).
2. Tom and you seem to be good friends? – Yes, we ________ (know) each other for a long time.
3. Our new car is great! We ________ (not have) any problems so far.
4. Oh, you've cleaned your bike! Why ________ (be) it so dirty yesterday?
5. It's five years now since I ________ (see) Dave.
6. The Chinese ________ (invent) printing.
7. They ________ (go) out after lunch and they've just come back home.
8. Jim ________ (live) in England for ten years. Now he lives in France.

You get 1 point for each correct answer. **Your points:** ________ /8

REMEMBER *Going to-future or will-future?*

Das *going to-future* benutzt man für Vorgänge, die unmittelbar bevorstehen.
Beispiel: "Be careful! That ladder is going to break."
Man verwendet es auch für feste Absichten.
Beispiel: I'm going to write to Peter as soon as I have a moment.

Das *will-future* benutzt man meist für Dinge, die man selbst nicht beeinflussen kann.
Beispiel: Rain will fall over Northern England during the night.
Man benutzt es auch für spontane Entschlüsse.
Beispiel: What flavour ice cream do you want? – I'll have strawberry.

3 Choose the correct form: will-future or going to-future.

1. The weather forecast said that rain ________ (spread) across southern England.
2. Oh, this shopping bag looks very heavy. I ________ (help) you with it.
3. What are your plans for tonight? I ________ (go) to the cinema with my parents.
4. I hope you ________ (win) the lottery with that ticket I bought for you.
5. I want to become rich, that's why I ________ (study) medicine and become a doctor.

You get 1 point for each correct answer. **Your points:** ________ /5

REMEMBER *Reported speech*

Die indirekte Rede (*reported speech*) wird immer mit einem Verb des Berichtens (say, tell, remind usw.) eingeleitet. Steht dieses im Präsens (z. B. says), so wird in der indirekten Rede die gleiche Zeitform benutzt wie in der direkten Rede.
Denke daran, dass du auch das Personalpronomen ändern musst.

Beispiel: Sarah: "You can't borrow my book, Peter."
→ Peter: "Sarah says I cannot borrow her book."
→ You: "Sarah says Peter cannot borrow her book."

4 What are the right forms for the verbs?

Mary is on the phone to her mum. Mrs Smith tells her husband what her daughter is saying.

EXAMPLE

Mary: "I'm going to be home late today."
Mrs Smith: "Mary says she *is going to be home* late today."

1. Mary: "I'm going to the cinema with my friend Angela."
   Mrs Smith: "Mary says she ______ to the cinema with her friend Angela."
2. Mary: "After the cinema we want to go shopping together."
   Mrs Smith: "After the cinema the girls ______ together".
3. Mary: "I really need a new shirt."
   Mrs Smith: " Mary informs us (that) she really ______ a new shirt."
4. Mr Smith: "She can buy one from her pocket money."
   Mrs Smith: "Your father lets you know (that) you ______ from your pocket money."
5. Mary: "But it's my birthday next week."
   Mrs Smith: "Mary reminds you ______."
6. Mr Smith: "OK, she can have it for her birthday then."
   Mrs Smith: "Dad says ______."
7. Mary: "Thank you mum and dad!"
   Mrs Smith: "Mary ______."

You get 1 point for each correct answer. **Your points:** ______ /7

REMEMBER *Question tags*

Mit *question tags* zeigt man, dass man das Gespräch weiterführen möchte und interessiert ist. Ist der Aussagesatz bejaht (I can), wird im *question tag* verneint (can't I?) und umgekehrt. Das Verb bleibt immer das Gleiche, außer im *simple past* (they went), wo wie bei Verneinungen das Hilfsverb benutzt wird (didn't they?).

5 Add the correct question tag.

It's Peter's first day at the new sports club. He has got lots of questions.

1. I can play basketball here, ______ ?
2. There aren't many girls here, ______ ?
3. There is a coach for the football team, ______ ?
4. You aren't allowed to wear normal shoes in the gym, ______ ?
5. You were at my school last year, ______ ?
6. But you haven't got a younger sister, ______ ?
7. The boys on that picture won the championship last year, ______ ?
8. I can't bring a friend for free, ______ ?

You get 1 point for each correct answer. **Your points:** ______ /8

6 Forming questions

Ask about the underlined words. Be careful with the tenses.

EXAMPLE

Lisa <u>played table-tennis</u> yesterday. → *What did Lisa do yesterday?*

1. School starts <u>on Monday</u>.
2. Thomas loves <u>his hamster Toby</u>.
3. <u>Toby</u> loves Thomas.
4. Peter visited <u>his grandfather</u> yesterday.
1. <u>Peter</u> visited his grandfather yesterday.
2. Peter visited his grandfather <u>yesterday</u>.
3. I usually go shopping <u>on Wednesdays</u>.
4. Luke went home <u>yesterday</u>.

You get 1 point for each correct answer. **Your points:** ______ /8

REMEMBER *Relative pronouns*

Who, which und that werden sowohl im Singular als auch im Plural gebraucht.
Who bezieht sich nur auf Personen, which nur auf Dinge. That kann für beides benutzt werden.
Whose ist der Genitiv (deren, dessen, siehe Beispiel unten).
Whom kann als Objekt im Relativsatz stehen, ist sehr förmlich und kann durch who/that ersetzt werden.
Wenn sich das Relativpronomen auf den ganzen vorherigen Satzteil (= vor dem Komma) bezieht (sog. *sentence relative*), muss which benutzt werden.

Beispiele: The man **who** built St. Paul's Cathedral is Christopher Wren.
The building **which** was built by Christopher Wren is St. Paul's Cathedral.
The woman **whose** child is playing in the yard is Mrs Green.
School in England only begins at 9 o'clock, **which** is amazing.

7 Fill in the correct relative pronoun.

1. I like films ______ have a happy ending.
2. What's the name of the teacher ______ book you borrowed?
3. Linda couldn't come with us to the park, ______ was a pity.
4. Some of the pupils ______ are in the class were ill yesterday.
5. The girls ______ are on the photo are my friends.
6. The city ______ I like best is London.
7. Where is the girl ______ pen you are using?
8. I enjoy doing sports ______ you can do in the water.

You get 1 point for each correct answer. **Your points:** ______ /8 points

8 Translate the following sentences. Use relative pronouns.
Achtung: Im Englischen steht kein Komma, im Deutschen schon!

1. Ich mag Geschichten, die mit Helden (= heroes) zu tun (= deal with) haben.
2. Die Menschen, deren Geschichten spannend sind, sind für mich die interessantesten.
3. Aber einige der Filme, die im Kino gezeigt werden, sind nicht gut.
4. Ich lese gerne Bücher, die nicht so dick sind.
5. Menschen, die nicht gerne lesen, verpassen (= miss) eine Menge.

You get 1 point for each correct answer. **Your points:** ______ /5 points

REMEMBER *Contact clauses*

Contact clauses können aus Nebensätzen gebildet werden, in denen die Relativpronomen nicht direkt vor den Verben stehen. Zwischen Relativpronomen und Verb steht entweder ein Personalpronomen (I, you, we, usw.) oder ein Name.

Beispiele: This is the book that I want to give to you.
He liked the film that he saw yesterday.

Bei allen Beispielen ist das Relativpronomen jetzt Objekt des Nebensatzes. Diese Relativsätze können ohne das Relativpronomen geschrieben werden:

This is the book I want to give to you.
He liked the film he saw yesterday.

Relative clause → This is the boy who I saw yesterday.
Contact clause → This is the boy I saw yesterday.

9 Make contact clauses. Make one sentence out of two sentences.

EXAMPLE

Peter is a boy. Everyone likes him. → *Peter is a boy everybody likes.*

1. The church is very old. You can see it over there.
2. Tummy is a cat. Mice don't like her.
3. The house is very big. It was built by my father.
4. This book is very interesting. I read it last year.
5. The "Mighty Micks" are a pop band. Only girls like them.
6. The cake is very good. Lynn made it.
7. The red sock is here. You were looking for it.

You get 1 point for each correct answer. Your points: ____ /7

REMEMBER *Conditional clauses*

Der Bedingungssatz Typ I drückt immer eine erfüllbare Bedingung aus (wenn ... dann). Im Nebensatz wird die Bedingung (if) beschrieben, im Hauptsatz das, was dann passiert (I will/you can usw.).

Achtung: Kein will oder would im *if*-Satz!
Beispiel: If the sun shines tomorrow, I will go to the swimming pool.

Folgt der Bedingungssatz auf den Hauptsatz, wird **kein** Komma gesetzt.

Beispiel: I will go swimming tomorrow if the sun shines.

10 Fill in the right form of the verb.

Tina and Dave are trying to raise money to rescue an old horse. They are talking about their ideas.

1. Tina: "If we ______ (ask) our teacher for help, he ______ (give) us some ideas."
2. Dave: "Our friends ______ (help) us if we ______ (explain) our plans to them."
3. Tina: "If we ______ (organize) a picnic, we ______ (have to) prepare a lot of food."
4. Dave: "That's true. But if we ______ (not get) enough money during the next five days, it ______ (be) too late for the horse."
5. Tina: "We can tell people about the horse in the newspaper! I ______ (take) some photos if you ______ (write) a report."

You get 1 point for each correct answer. Your points: ______ /10

REMEMBER *Modal auxiliaries: might*

Achtung: Das Hilfsverb might drückt aus, dass etwas sehr unsicher ist.
Beispiel: He might be right. – He could be right.
Beide Sätze werden mit „Er könnte Recht haben." übersetzt, in dem Satz mit might ist sich der Sprecher jedoch unsicherer als in dem Satz mit could.

11 Fill in these modal auxiliaries:

shall/should	*may/might*	*can/could*
soll/sollte	mag/könnte	kann/könnte

1. Dave: "__________ I bring you your jacket, Tina?" (Soll ...?)
2. Tina: "No, thanks, but you __________ bring me my shoes." (könntest)
3. Dave: "You __________ also want to put on some socks first!" (Vielleicht möchtest du ...?)
4. Tina: "Oh dear, I didn't know I wasn't wearing socks. I really __________ lose my head one day." (Eines Tages könnte ich wirklich mal meinen Kopf vergessen.)
5. Dave: "__________ I remind you of what you forgot last week?" (Soll ...?)
6. Tina: "No, please not, or I __________ start to cry." (oder ich fange vielleicht an zu weinen)
7. Tina: "But I __________ tell you a nice story that happened to my friend last week." (könnte)
8. Dave: "Well, I think we really __________ go now. We're late!" (sollten)

You get 1 point for each correct answer. **Your points:** __________ /8

REMEMBER *Some – any – no and their compounds*

In bejahten Sätzen verwendet man Zusammensetzungen mit some.
In Fragen und verneinten Aussagesätzen verwendet man any.
Zusammensetzungen können z. B. folgende Worte sein:
somebody / anybody / nobody
something / anything / nothing
somewhere / anywhere / nowhere

12 In the hospital. Decide which is the best word here.

1. "I have just seen __________ in the corridor. Who was it?"
2. "Oh, I think it was __________ doctor. Usually there is __________ (keiner) out there."
3. "I'll go to the newsagent's to buy a drink. Do you need __________?"
4. "Yes, please bring me __________ to read."
5. "Do you want __________ special?"
6. "I would like __________ fashion magazine, please. But don't go __________ too far for it."
7. "I'm back. Sorry, there was __________ fashion magazine left. And there wasn't __________ other shop."
8. "That's OK. I have __________ old ones. They must be __________ over there. They're better than __________."

You get 1 point for each correct answer. **Your points:** __________ /13

REMEMBER *Adjective – adverb*

Adjektive beschreiben ein Nomen näher (She is a quick learner.), sie stehen nach dem Verb to be oder vor einem Substantiv.
Adverbien beziehen sich meistens auf ein Verb (She learns quickly.), sie stehen nach dem Vollverb, dem erstem Hilfsverb oder einem Objekt. Sie werden meist aus Adjektiven gebildet, an die man ein -ly anhängt.
Adverbien können sich auch auf Adjektive oder andere Adverbien beziehen.
Beispiele: You're looking extremely good today.
You learned that remarkably well.
Steigerung: Einsilbige Adverbien werden wie einsilbige Adjektive mit -er und -est gesteigert. Mehrsilbige Adverbien werden wie mehrsilbige Adjektive mit more und most gesteigert.

13 Complete each sentence with a word from the list.
Be careful: sometimes you need the adjective (careful etc.) and sometimes the adverb (carefully etc.)

careful(ly) *complete(ly)* *happy/happily* *nervous(ly)* *quick(ly)*

1. We have to go home. Our free time passed very ______.
2. Be ______. The dog bites.
3. Alice and Tom are very ______ married. They smile all the time.
4. The pupils were very quiet. There was ______ silence during the lesson.
5. I don't like exams. I'm usually very ______ the day before.
6. This is a baby, not a doll. You have to touch it more ______.
7. The policeman stopped her. What did he want from her? She was very upset and opened the car door ______.
8. I've got to go out in five minutes. Could you make me a ______ sandwich?
9. There is not a single right answer here. The homework is ______ wrong.
10. Look at David and his dog. They look very ______. They are really having fun.

You get 1 point for each correct answer. Your points: ______ /10

REMEMBER *to + infinitive*

Sätze klingen im Englischen oft besser, wenn sie mit einer Infinitivkonstruktion gebildet werden.

Beispiel: We watched the school's musical last year. It was fantastic!
→ It was fantastic **to watch** the school's musical last year!

14 Back at school after the holidays

The summer holidays are over and there is a lot to tell. Lucy and her friends are talking about all the important news of the new school year.
Put these sentences together with to + infinitive. You always have to start with the second sentence.

1. We watched the basketball match last night. It was exciting.
2. Let's go to the maths lesson now. It's time.
3. Play your card, Simon. It's your turn.
4. Tell everybody about the new project. It's important.
5. Tina can't play the piano. She is going to learn it.
6. Some pupils are collecting money for charity. They started last week.

You get 1 point for each correct answer. Your points: ____ /6

15 The class party

Lucy and her friends are planning a party on the school grounds for their class. To invite everyone, they want to put up a poster. Part of the poster is missing. Use to + infinitive. Choose verbs from the list.

to + *come* *bring* *write to* *help*

Class party for Mrs Whitehead's class

1. When ____ : At 4 p.m. on Friday. Don't be late!
2. What ____ : Food, drink, games
3. How ____ : Give us your ideas for games.
4. Who ____ : Lucy and Carol: LaC@bird.net.uk

You get 1 point for each correct answer. Your points: ____ /4

Your total points out of 128 points: ____

If you have less than 57 points you should look at the book for year 6 again. That will make it easier for you to do the exercises in this book.

2 Sprache verstehen

Das solltest du am Ende der Klasse 7 können:

- An Gesprächen teilnehmen und über vertraute Inhalte zusammenhängend sprechen
- Besonders in Alltagssituationen deine Absichten mitteilen, in der Zielsprache auf andere Menschen reagieren sowie Gesprächsinhalte wiedergeben
- Sach- und Gebrauchstexte ins Englische übertragen

REMEMBER *Active voice and passive voice*

Aktivsätze betonen, wer etwas tut.
Passivsätze betonen hingegen, was getan wird. Die Handlung selbst steht im Vordergrund. Wer etwas getan hat, ist nicht so wichtig.

Beispiele:
A: **Somebody** took my English book last lesson.
→ Jemand nahm letzte Stunde mein Englischbuch.
P: My English book **was taken** last lesson.
→ Mein Englischbuch wurde letzte Stunde (weg)genommen.

Im Aktivsatz (A) ist somebody das Subjekt und wird daher betont.
Im Passivsatz (P) hingegen liegt die Betonung auf my English book, daher ist diese Wortgruppe das Subjekt in diesem Satz.

- Im Aktivsatz ist das Subjekt aktiv, es tut etwas.
- Anders als in einem Aktivsatz tut das Subjekt des Passivsatzes nichts, sondern etwas passiert mit ihm.
- In vielen Passivsätzen ist entweder unbekannt oder sogar unwichtig, wer die Handlungen verursacht hat. Oder es ist so offensichtlich, dass der „Täter“ nicht extra genannt werden muss.
- Wenn man trotzdem den Verursacher der Handlung nennen will (von wem etwas gemacht wird), benutzt man die Präposition by (auf Deutsch: von). Dieser Verursacher der Handlung wird by-agent genannt.
- Passivsätze findet man vor allem in Zeitungsberichten, technischen Beschreibungen und historischen Texten.
- Ein englischer Passivsatz wird im Deutschen oft mit „man“ übersetzt, z. B. „Man hat mir mein Englischbuch weggenommen.“

Bildung des Passivs:

- Das Passiv wird immer gebildet mit einer Form von to be und dem *past participle*. Die Form von to be wird der jeweiligen Zeitstufe angepasst.
- Nach will oder einem Modalverb (can, must usw.) wird die **Passivform des Infinitivs** verwendet → be + *past participle* → Your parents **must be** informed.
- Passivsätze können in verschiedenen Zeitformen vorkommen.
- Passivsätze kann man nur mit Verben bilden, denen ein Objekt folgt (transitive Verben), z. B. to build (a house), to visit (a friend), to watch (a film), usw.
- Passivsätze können sowohl mit der *simple* als auch mit der *progressive* Form des Verbs gebildet werden. → He **was caught** last Thursday by the police. But he escaped while he **was being taken** to the police station.

Hier ist eine Übersicht mit Beispielen für die Passivformen:

simple present	→ am/is/are + *past participle*
The Tower of London **is visited** by many tourists from all over the world.	→ ... wird ... besucht ...
Tours **are given** regularly by guides.	→ ... werden ... gegeben.
simple past	→ was/were + *past participle*
It **was used** for many different purposes: as a castle, as a prison, as a museum ...	→ ... wurde ... benutzt ...
The prisoners **weren't treated** very well.	→ ... wurden nicht ... behandelt.
present perfect	→ has/have been + *past participle*
A new exhibition on the Tower's prisoners **has** just **been announced** in the newspaper.	→ ... ist ... angekündigt worden.
Have you **been told** about it by your teacher?	→ Bist du/Seid ihr ... von ... informiert worden?
future passive	→ will be + *past participle*
The exhibition **will be opened** next Saturday.	→ ... wird ... eröffnet (werden).
And it **won't be closed** until the end of the summer holidays.	→ ... wird nicht ... geschlossen (werden).

1 Put in passive forms: *present* or *past* or *present perfect*. Signal words (see box below) can help you.

Be clever: Don't buy this book! It ________ already ________ (call) the silliest book that ________ ever ________ (publish) – and I think that's true!
Aliens in the Tower ________ (write) in 2007 by Seamus Strolph. He said in an interview that the idea for the book ________ (give) to him during his last visit to London when he ________ (tell) by a guide (= Führer) about the history of prisoners in the Tower of London. Just to get this right, I think the Tower is an interesting topic. I just don't understand how the history of this ancient castle could ________ (turn) into such a story.
Listen to this: We are in the year 2199 and strange things are happening in the Tower. The wardens soon find out that an alien ________ (send) to the earth some months ago. But they don't know who the alien is because human bodies ________ (use) by the alien as a disguise (= Verkleidung). When they finally find the deadly alien, many prisoners ________ (kill), parts of the Tower of London ________ (destroy) and the reader ________ ________ (bore) almost to death, because nearly five hundred pages ________ (waste) on this far-fetched (= an den Haaren herbeigezogenen) story. Don't waste your time and money! Believe me, books like that ________ just ________ (make) for the bin!

REMEMBER *Signal words*

Hier findest du eine Liste wichtiger Signalwörter für die Zeiten in der linken Spalte:

tense	***signal words***
simple present	every day, often, never, always, regularly, sometimes, usually, on Sundays, in the afternoons
simple past	in 1996, yesterday, some years ago, last night, after breakfast, a few days ago, in the past, during his visit
present perfect	yet, already, ever, just (now), never, not ... yet, so far, often

Achtung: Adverbien wie already, never usw. stehen im *present perfect* immer nach dem ersten Hilfsverb.

Beispiel: This story has already been written.

1 At the Tower of London

Here are some rules which can be seen at the gate of the Tower of London. Write the verb phrases in English. Remember that the *passive infinitive* is used after modal verbs.

1. Cars ______
   (müssen geparkt werden) in the official car park.
2. Bags ______
   (können hinterlassen werden) in the cloakroom.
3. Souvenirs ______
   (können gekauft werden) at the souvenir shop.
4. Photos
   (dürfen nicht gemacht werden = take) inside the White Tower.
5. Children ______
   (müssen begleitet werden = accompany) by an adult.

2 The Crown Jewels have been stolen!

One of the reasons why so many tourists visit the Tower of London each year is to see the Crown Jewels. They are shown in the White Tower. Even though there is a lot of security, people are always afraid that they might be stolen one day.
Rewrite these active sentences and make them passive. Use the simple past form of the passive. Leave out the by-agent.

EXAMPLE

(They) stole the Crown Jewels yesterday.
→ *The Crown Jewels were stolen yesterday.*

1. (The police officers) questioned visitors to the Tower.
2. (No one) saw the thieves.
3. (The security men) watched all the video tapes from that day.
4. (The chief inspector) checked the criminal records (= Verbrecherkartei).
5. (The police) arrested two men last night.
6. (The police) searched the houses of the suspects.
7. (An officer) found the Crown Jewels in the cellar.
8. (The chief inspector) informed the director of the museum.
9. (The director of the museum) reopened the exhibition of the Crown Jewels this morning.
10. (The judge = Richter) sent the thieves to prison.

3 A tour of the Tower of London

Fill in the gaps. You have to decide: active or passive voice? But be careful, you have to fill in many different tenses.

1. Guide: Welcome to the Tower of London. On this tour you ______ (inform) about everything there is to know about the Tower.
2. Let's start with the history of the Tower. After his conquest of England in 1066, William the Conqueror ______ (start) to build impressive castles all over the country. Among these fortifications ______ (be) the White Tower in London, the first of the twenty towers which ______ (belong) to what ______ (call) the "Tower of London" nowadays.
3. The White Tower, which ______ (complete) in 1078, was the strongest and most fearsome Norman fortification in the whole country. In the past it ______ (mean) to strengthen the River Thames against attacks from enemies and it ______ (protect) the Royal Family from the people of London in times of disorder. Not only the shape and size of the Tower but also its purpose ______ (change) over the centuries.
4. Before the Middle Ages the castle ______ (mainly/use) for residential and military functions. Between the 14th and 19th century the Royal Mint, the Crown Jewels and the King's menagerie, an assortment of wild and exotic animals, ______ (also/house = unterbringen) in the Tower.
5. From the 14th to the 17th century the Tower ______ (use) as a prison. Especially in the 15th and 16th century it ______ (become) a scene of torture, murder and executions. Its prisoners ______ (include) criminals, as well as unpopular aristocrats and even members of the Royal Family, who ______ (imprison = einsperren) for reasons of power.
6. ______ you ______ (see) the ravens when you ______ (walk) around the White Tower? Ravens ______ (become) part of the Tower in the 17th century. A legend says that should the ravens ever leave the Tower of London something bad ______ (happen) to England and its people. Of course we don't want this to happen, which is why, even today, six or seven ravens ______ (still/keep) and ______ (look after) in the Tower grounds.

REMEMBER *Reflexive pronouns and reflexive verbs*

Reflexivpronomen beziehen sich auf das Subjekt des Satzes **zurück.**

→ Die Singularformen der englischen Reflexivpronomen enden auf -self, die Pluralformen auf -selves.

Beispiele:
She hurt herself. They dressed **themselves**.
Shall I help you with your homework? – No, thank you. I can do it **myself**.
Tina's dress looks nice. – Yes, it does, and she made it **herself**.
I won't be here tomorrow evening, children, so you'll have to look after **yourselves**.

- ▶ Den Reflexivpronomen im Englischen entspricht im Deutschen: mich/mir (selbst), dich/dir (selbst), sich (selbst) usw.
- ▶ Mit den Pronomen auf -self/-selves kannst du betonen, dass jemand etwas selbst tut. Diese Pronomen stehen meist am Satzende.

Das Reflexivpronomen kommt im Englischen viel seltener vor als im Deutschen. Vielen Verben, die im Deutschen mit **„sich"** gebildet werden, entspricht im Englischen ein nicht reflexives Verb. Diese Verben musst du in der Regel einfach auswendig lernen.
Beispiel: I haven't seen you for a long time. You have changed a lot. (*Not reflexive*).
→ Ich habe dich eine ganze Weile nicht gesehen. Du hast **dich** sehr **verändert**.

Hier siehst du Verben, die im Deutschen reflexiv sind, im Englischen aber nicht:

sich verändern	to change	sich erinnern	to remember
sich anziehen	to get dressed	sich fühlen	to feel
sich beeilen	to hurry	sich öffnen	to open
sich bewegen	to move	sich (hin)setzen	to sit down
sich entscheiden	to decide	sich treffen	to meet
sich entspannen	to relax	sich trennen	to split up
sich ereignen	to happen	sich verirren	to get lost

Im Deutschen kann man **„sich"** außerdem im Sinne von „einander" oder „sich gegenseitig" gebrauchen. Im Englischen wird in dieser Bedeutung kein Reflexivpronomen, sondern each other verwendet.
Beispiele:
They know each other. → Sie kennen sich (gegenseitig).
We gave each other a mobile. → Wir haben uns gegenseitig ein Handy gegeben.

1 Fill in the correct reflexive pronouns.
Lucy sometimes works as a babysitter to increase (=aufbessern) her pocket money. Today she is spending the afternoon with Mrs Alexander's children, Tony, Katy and Jimmy.

1. Lucy: When you've all made ____________ comfortable, I'll read you a story.
2. Tony: I need a plaster Lucy! I have cut ____________.
3. Lucy: Oh dear, how did you cut ____________?

4. Tony: It's Jimmy's fault. He was the doctor and I was the patient. He told me to hold the instruments for the operation. But the knife was real. How can he call ________ a doctor? Now I really am hurt.
5. Katy: Lucy, why do mummies feed their babies?
   Lucy: Because little babies can't feed ________, Katy.
6. Katy: But a baby-bird doesn't have to be fed, because it can eat ________.
7. Lucy: Yes, that's right. Oh, we have to meet your mother in the park in twenty minutes. It's time for us to get ________ ready.
8. Tony: Didn't you hear what Lucy said, Jimmy? Get dressed, or do you think she was just talking to ________?

2 Fill in the reflexive pronouns.

While Lucy is looking after the children, Mrs Alexander is meeting her friends. They all have children, so they call themselves the "Mummies Club". When they meet they usually talk about lots of different things.

1. What about the party next Saturday? Have we got something that the children can do? They want to make ________ useful (= sich nützlich machen).
2. Betty! Mathilda! You two look great! Have you bought ________ (euch) new clothes?
3. Swimming lessons? No, Glenn didn't have a teacher. He taught ________ (sich selbst) to swim.
4. Why work? This is a question I ask ________ (mich selbst) every time I have to pay the nanny. It would be cheaper for me to stay at home ________.
5. I don't like my new neighbour. She only thinks about ________ (sich).
6. But I think your neighbour invited you for dinner in that expensive restaurant? – Invited us? No, we paid for ________ (uns selbst).

3 Put in the right verb from the list below.

When all the mothers talk to each other at the same time, it is sometimes very hard to listen to them. So Mrs Alexander gets to know lots of gossip (= Klatsch und Tratsch) while listening to different conversations at the same time.

complain *meet* *get divorced* *wonder/ask myself* *hurry* *feel*

"Believe me, the service there is awful. I'm going to ________ "–
"Oh, then I won't go there!"
"Linda, you always know everything about everyone. We really must ________ more often."
"Did you know? Carol and Jeremy have decided to ________ "– "Really? They seemed to be the perfect couple!"

"I ______ what he'll say when I tell him. What do you think? How would your husband react?"
"I told them 'We're going to be late. We must ______', but you know my children. We missed the film in the end."
"Being single again is super. I ______ great!"

4 Lucy's "Babysitter Club"

Lucy liked the idea of Mrs Alexander's "Mummies Club", so she founded a club for babysitters. Once a month all the babysitters meet and discuss what happened to them while they were babysitting. They also help each other when there are problems. This month there are a lot of new boys and girls at the meeting.

Complete the sentences. Fill in the English reflexive pronoun or leave a blank space. How do you translate the German reflexive pronoun "sich"? You have to decide: *herself*, *himself*, *ourselves* or *each other*?

Lucy: Oh, hello Sarah! Come in and make ______ comfortable (sich bequem machen). You can sit ______ (sich hinsetzen) down here.
Sarah: Thank you. Wow, I wouldn't have thought you'd remember ______ (sich erinnern) what my name is.
Lucy: Well, that was easy. I don't think you two know ______ (sich kennen). Let me introduce you. Sarah, this is Peter.
Sarah: Peter? Of course! We went to school together. I almost didn't recognize you, Peter. You have changed ______ (sich verändern) a lot.
Fiona: You want to know what the little boy did afterwards? Well, he looked at ______ (sich anschauen) in the mirror (= Spiegel) and started to cry!
Peggy: Oh no! Naughty (= ungezogen) boy! You said you might not want to go there again. When are you going to decide ______ (sich entscheiden)?
Fiona: I have decided already! I won't go there again. You can go from now on if you want to. But let me warn you, the mother always worries ______ (sich Sorgen machen) that something bad is going to happen while she is away.
Peggy: By the way, is Ann okay? Or did she hurt ______ (sich verletzen) when she fell down the stairs?

REMEMBER *Adjectives and adverbs*

Ein **Adjektiv** gibt an, **wie** eine Person oder Sache **ist**.
Du weißt, dass Adjektive ein Substantiv näher bestimmen. Es gibt jedoch eine Reihe von Verben, denen ein Adjektiv folgt.

Adjektive nach bestimmten Verben und Adverbien
Ein Adjektiv steht entweder vor einem Nomen (Beispiel: They play cool music.) oder nach dem Verb to be (Beispiel: This radio station **is cool.**).
Adverbien hingegen gehören meistens **zum Verb** und geben an, **wie** jemand etwas **tut** oder wie etwas **geschieht**. (Beispiel: The dog **ate** its food **hungrily**.) Man bildet sie mit -ly.
Adverbien können auch Adjektive oder andere Adverbien weiter bestimmen.
Beispiele: She is a **highly** successful artist.
I thought him **extremely** rude.
Jim ran **unusually** fast.

Es gibt jedoch einige Verben, denen ein Adjektiv statt eines Adverbs folgt. Dazu gehören:

- **Eigenschafts- oder Zustandsverben:**
  Die Verben be, seem, feel und stay verweisen auf einen Zustand oder eine Eigenschaft. Daher steht nach ihnen ein Adjektiv.
  Become und get entsprechen dem deutschen Wort „werden". Ihnen folgt ebenso ein Adjektiv.

- **Verben der Sinneswahrnehmung:**
  Look, smell, sound und taste drücken Sinneswahrnehmungen aus. Auch nach ihnen steht ein Adjektiv.

Beispiele:
Shona **was** a little **worried** when she arrived in Germany. Everything **seemed** so **strange** to her. But soon she **felt better**. She **became familiar** with the country. The German food **smelt** and **looked interesting** and **tasted wonderful**. Only the names of the dishes still **sound unusual** to her today.
Shona war zuerst ein wenig beunruhigt, als sie nach Deutschland kam. Alles erschien ihr so seltsam. Aber sie fühlte sich schnell besser. Sie wurde vertraut mit dem Land. Das deutsche Essen roch und sah interessant aus und schmeckte wunderbar. Nur die Namen der Gerichte hören sich für sie immer noch ungewohnt an.

1 Adjective or adverb? Fill in the correct form.
Mrs Alexander is talking to her husband about their first meeting.

You must remember that evening. We met at a ____________ (big) party at Ann's house. I was standing ____________ (quiet) at the buffet, and I was ____________ (slow) getting full (= satt), when you came for a ____________ (quick) snack. You said: "The food smells ____________ (good)" and ate a lot. We started to talk and you asked me to dance. You were dancing ____________ (wild) most of the time, so you were very ________ (thirsty). When you went to the bar, someone next to you ________ (stupid) knocked their glass over. You ________ (automatic) took a step backwards and stepped on my foot. It all happened so ________ (sudden). I was already quite ________ (drunk) and I ________ (simple) threw my drink at you. You ________ (probable) wanted to hit me, but you behaved so ________ (polite). You said, “Oh, your glass is empty. Let me get you another drink”.

REMEMBER *Adverbien mit Sonderformen*

Nicht alle Adverbien werden durch das Anhängen von -ly gebildet. Einige haben besondere Formen.
Zu dem Adjektiv good gehört das Adverb well.
Einige Adverbien haben die gleiche Form wie das Adjektiv.
Beispiele: early, fast, late, hard
Nicht verwechseln: late (spät) – lately (in letzter Zeit)
hard (hart, schwer) – hardly (kaum)

2 Mr Alexander is telling his mother about his job.
Fill the correct form (adjective or adverb) in the gap.

1. I haven’t had much free time ________ (late/lately).
2. I’ve been working very ________ (hard/hardly) at the office.
3. Life has been ________ (extreme/extremely) stressful.
4. I’ve ________ (hard/hardly) had a moment to myself.
5. I am ________ (awful/awfully) tired.
6. I am also becoming ________ (terrible/terribly) boring. I can only talk about work!

3 Lucy takes the ‘Babysitter Exam’.
An agency that places (= vermitteln an) babysitters with parents offers young babysitters the opportunity to take a babysitting course and ‘Babysitter Exam’. In the course you learn to read stories, to look after the children and care for light injuries (= Verletzungen versorgen). Lots of parents feel better if they know their babysitter has taken that course. After the exam the examiner talks to Lucy.
Fill in *good* or *well*.

Examiner: "I thought you were ______. You read the story very ______."

Lucy: "Thank you. It's a ______ book for children. The author writes extremely ______."

Lucy: "But I think I didn't explain how to look after injuries very ______. It wasn't a very ______ explanation."

Examiner: "You answered that question ______. That was very ______, because you received two extra points for the answer. Don't worry, Lucy. You'll be a ______ babysitter."

Lucy: "Thank you. It is very ______ to hear that from an examiner!"

After the exam Lucy tells her friend Fiona about it:

Fiona: "Lucy! Was the exam ______? Did it go ______?"

Lucy: "Yes, the exam went ______. I was ______ prepared. I'm so happy now!"

Fiona: "And what about the families they place you with. Do they pay ______ money?"

Lucy: "No, the money is not ______. I'll keep my old families. They always paid me very ______."

4 Lucy receives a postcard.

Translate into English. Use the adverbs and adjectives of the following words.

bad *happy* *perfect*

Liebe Lucy,

1. Bist du in deiner neuen Schule glücklich?
2. Das Meer ist toll in Italien. Tony ist ein perfekter Schwimmer.
3. Wir sind nun in einer Ferienwohnung (= holiday apartment), denn es war ein sehr schlechtes Hotel.
4. Katy und Jimmy haben dort sehr schlecht geschlafen, weil es so laut war.
5. Aber die Kinder haben sich sehr gut benommen (= behave).
6. Der Kellner (= waiter) lächelte immer sehr glücklich, wenn er sie essen sah (= when he saw them eating).
7. Es ist der perfekte Urlaub für uns.
8. Die Kinder sind glücklich, das Essen ist gut, nur Herr Alexander hat schlechte Laune (= to be in a ... mood). Er hat einen Sonnenbrand (= sunburn).

Viele Grüße

Katy, Jimmy, Tony und Herr & Frau Alexander

REMEMBER *The future tense*

Das Futur kann auf verschiedene Art und Weise ausgedrückt werden. Die unterschiedlichen Möglichkeiten werden hier aufgeführt.

Futur I *(will-* and ***going to-future)***
Bei der Verwendung des Futur I wird im Englischen zwischen zwei Formen unterschieden, dem ***will-*** und ***going to-future***.

will-future
- spontaner Entschluss
- Meinung, Hoffnung, Vermutung
- nicht beeinflussbares Versprechen

going to-future
- vorbereitete, geplante Handlung
- logische Schlussfolgerung
- unmittelbar bevorstehende Vorgänge

Beide Formen werden mit dem Infinitiv eines Verbs gebildet.

Beispiele:

Wait, I **will** help you.
(spontaner Entschluss)

I **am going** to study harder next year.
(festes Vorhaben)

Verwendung von Gegenwartsformen für die Zukunft
In bestimmten Situationen kannst du auch Formen der Gegenwart verwenden, um zukünftiges Geschehen auszudrücken.

Das ***simple present*** wird bei festgelegten und feststehenden Handlungen (z. B. Fahrplan, Programm, Hotels) in der Zukunft verwendet.
Beispiel: The train leaves at 9 a.m.

Das ***present progressive*** wird bei Handlungen verwendet, die bereits für einen Zeitpunkt in der Zukunft vereinbart sind. Es wird aus dem Zusammenhang klar, dass es hier um eine zukünftige Handlung geht. Manchmal verweist eine temporale bzw. lokale Ergänzung auf die Zukunft.
Beispiele: I am meeting him next week/outside the theatre.
We're having lunch together after the meeting.

Futur II (*future perfect* – vollendete Zukunft)
Das Futur II (vollendete Zukunft) drückt im Englischen aus, dass eine Handlung zu einem Zeitpunkt in der Zukunft abgeschlossen sein wird.
Dieser Zeitpunkt wird häufig durch eine Zeitangabe wie by the end of next week, by Friday, by July etc. festgelegt.

Das *future perfect* wird gebildet mit will/won't + have + *past participle.*
Beispiel: Tom: Will she have landed by this time next week?
Greg: Yes, she will (have). (Oder: Yes, by this time next week she will have landed in Ireland.)

1 Use the words in brackets and transfer them into the *future perfect* form.

EXAMPLE

By 12 o'clock we ___ (cook) lunch.
→ By 12 o'clock we *will have cooked* lunch.

1. My grandparents ___ (eat) by then.
2. In three months Billy ___ (cross) the Pacific by boat.
3. By this time tomorrow, you ___ (write) the test.
4. The sun ___ (not/rise) by 5 o'clock.
5. ___ you ___ (do) the laundry (= Wäsche waschen) by this afternoon? I really need my shirt tonight!
6. By 2025 astronauts ___ (fly) to the moon many more times.
7. Do you think that you ___ (buy) yourself a car by your twentieth birthday?

2 Tom and Greg talk about what they need to do.

Tom is going on holidays next week. Until then he has some things to do. He is telling his friend Greg about it. Fill in the gaps using the *future perfect* form.

EXAMPLE

Tom: I ___ (repair) my bike by next week.
→ Tom: I *will have repaired* my bike by next week.

1. Tom: Listen Greg, I ___ (pack) my suitcase by next week. And I ___ (do) the washing by Friday.
2. In two weeks time from now I still ___ (not come) back. I ___ (not be) on the final part of my trip yet. As far as I know I ___ (return) by August 4th, which is four weeks from now.
3. By the time of my return, I ___ (be) in a few English-speaking countries. I ___ (be) to Ireland and Iceland. – What ___ (do) by then, Greg?
4. Greg: I don't know exactly what I ___ (do) by then. Maybe I ___ (visit) London. But our trip ___ (finish) a long time before yours. As far as I know we ___ (already leave) London a week before your return.
5. Tom: London sounds great, too. I'll know more about it tomorrow. By then ___ (write) a paper about it. It's our homework and I haven't even started yet. I need to go. See you later!

3 Lisa and Betty's bus ride

Lisa and Betty are close friends. On their way home from school they are talking about their future. Watch out, *Futur I* forms might also be possible. And notice that in time clauses, like in 'if' clauses, the future is not used!

EXAMPLE

Lisa: By the age of 21 I ________ (fall in love = sich verlieben), I'm sure.
Lisa: By the age of 21 I *will have fallen in love,* I'm sure.

1. Betty: I guess I ________ (meet) the man of my dreams a lot earlier than at the age of 21.
   But I think it might be a bit longer before I move out of my parents' house because they are so important to me. It's easy to live with them, because by the time I move out I ________ (save) a lot of money on rent. (= Miete)
2. Lisa: Well, you are right. I am sure that I ________ (be) to Australia by the time I move out. It's something that I ________ (do) by the age of 18.
   A High School year is very appealing (= vielversprechend).
3. Betty: Oh, that's something I ________ also ________ (do) by the time I'm 20. I am not sure about Australia though, maybe it ________ (be) the USA or Canada. - I don't know yet.
4. Lisa: That sounds great, too. What about children? I am sure that I ________ ________ (have) a couple of kids by the age of 30. I think it's a good age.
5. Betty: Oh no! I don't think that I ________ (have) children until I'm 35.
   That seems fine with me. – Lisa, my stop is coming up shortly. See you soon!
   Lisa: Bye ... See you soon!

REMEMBER *Conditional clauses* – Bedingungssätze

Ein Bedingungssatz besteht immer aus einem if-Satz (*if-clause*) und einem Hauptsatz (*main clause*). Der if-Satz beschreibt eine Bedingung und der Hauptsatz drückt aus, was passieren wird oder passieren könnte, wenn diese Bedingung erfüllt wird.
Es gibt drei Grundtypen von Bedingungssätzen:
Typ 1: Der Sprecher hält die Bedingung für erfüllbar.
Typ 2: Der Sprecher zweifelt an der Erfüllbarkeit der Bedingung.
Typ 3: Der Sprecher weiß, dass die Bedingung nicht mehr erfüllt werden kann, z. B. weil die Situation bereits in der Vergangenheit liegt.

Conditional Clause Type I

Bei Typ 1 steht die erfüllbare Bedingung im if-Satz immer im *simple present*. Die Folge der Bedingung steht im Hauptsatz und wird meist mit dem *will-future* gebildet.

Neben dem ***will-future*** werden im Hauptsatz auch häufig modale Hilfsverben wie z. B. can, must, needn't oder der Imperativ verwendet.

Bedingungssätze können mit dem if-Satz oder dem Hauptsatz beginnen.
Beispiele:
If you need some help, ask Dad. → Komma vor dem Hauptsatz.
Ask Dad if you need some help. → Kein Komma vor dem if-Satz.

Erfüllbare Bedingung im if-Satz: ***Simple present***	Folge im Hauptsatz: ***will-future***
If Louise **goes** to bed late,	she **will be** tired tomorrow.
If you **repair** the bike,	you **will be** able to ride it to school.
If that **doesn't work,**	we **must** buy a new bike.

Conditional Clause Type II
Bei Typ 2 steht die erfüllbare Bedingung im if-Satz im *simple past*. Die Folge im Hauptsatz wird meist mit dem *conditional* (would + *infinitive*) gebildet.
Du verwendest Typ 2, wenn du daran zweifelst, dass die Bedingung erfüllbar ist, oder wenn du genau weißt, dass sie nicht erfüllt werden kann.

Das *simple past* im if-Satz drückt hier nicht aus, dass die Handlung in der Vergangenheit stattfand, sondern beschreibt eine unwahrscheinliche oder unmögliche Bedingung.
Beispiel:
If I were you ... → Wenn ich du wäre ...
→ Neben dem ***conditional*** (would + *infinitive*) kannst du im Hauptsatz auch could/might + *infinitive* gebrauchen.
Beispiel:
If I had lots of money, I could buy an island.
→ Wenn ich eine Menge Geld hätte, könnte ich eine Insel kaufen.

Achtung: Anders als im Deutschen darf im if-Satz nie das *conditional* stehen.
→ Verwende niemals would, could, might usw. im if-Satz!

Nur theoretisch erfüllbare Bedingung im if-Satz: ***simple past***	Folge im Hauptsatz: ***conditional*** (would + ***infinitive***)
If your bike **wasn't broken,**	you **could ride** it to school.
Wenn dein Rad nicht kaputt wäre,	könntest du damit in die Schule fahren.
If you **had** a new bike,	there **wouldn't be** any problems.
Wenn du ein neues Rad hättest,	gäbe es keine Probleme./ würde es keine Probleme geben.
If I **were** you,	**I'd buy** a new one.
Wenn ich an deiner Stelle wäre,	würde ich ein neues kaufen.

1 Plans for the next class trip

As soon as Louise and her classmates returned from their trip, they started to plan the next one. Many pupils had good ideas, but most of them were very unrealistic.
Put the verbs in the right form: *simple past* or *would/could + infinitive*.

1. Tim: If we ______ (have) enough money, we ______ (go) to America.
2. Lewis: Yes, and ______ I ______ (be) the emperor of China I ______ (pay) for all of you!
3. Ginny: But what about Scotland? We ______ (go) cycling there ______ the weather ______ (be) nice in autumn.
4. Chris: Yeah, right. And ______ (we/be) lucky if it ______ (only rain) every second day.
5. Louise: What a pity. ______ (we all/be) over sixteen years old ______ (we/go) rock climbing.
6. Peter: We only ______ (go) rock climbing ______ (everyone/be) as sporty as you, Louise.
7. Louise: ______ (I/be) you Peter, I ______ (eat) less chocolate. Then doing sports would be more fun.
8. Tina: ______ (boys/not be) against it, ______ (I/like) to stay at a farm. You can do horse-riding there.
9. Marlon: ______ (I/never/touch) a horse even ______ (give) me a lot of money!
10. Mrs Robinson: And I ______ (go) anywhere with you ______ (you/not be) arguing all the time!

REMEMBER *Conditional clause type III*

Bei Typ 3 steht die nicht mehr erfüllbare Bedingung im if-Satz im *past perfect*. Die Folge im Hauptsatz muss *conditional perfect* (would + have + *past participle*) sein.

Du verwendest Typ 3, wenn du weißt, dass die Bedingung nicht mehr erfüllt werden kann, weil es sich um eine abgeschlossene Situation handelt, die in der Vergangenheit stattgefunden hat (aber siehe auch die Beispiele unten für weitere Situationen). Der Bedingungssatz Typ 3 wird daher benutzt, wenn du sagen möchtest, wie eine Situation sein könnte, wenn etwas anderes passiert wäre.

Beispiel:
If you had not broken your bike, your parents would not have bought you a new one.
→ Wenn du dein Fahrrad nicht kaputt gemacht hättest, hätten dir deine Eltern kein neues gekauft.

Wo im englischen if-Satz das *past perfect* steht, findest du im Deutschen eine Konjunktivform (z. B. gefragt hätten, gewesen wäre, gewusst hätte).
Auch im Konditional Typ 3 kannst du neben would auch could oder might benutzen.

Achtung: Bei den Kurzformen musst du aufpassen:
-'d kann die Kurzform von had und von would sein.
Aus dem Satzzusammenhang kannst du erkennen, um welche Form es sich handelt.
Beispiele:
I'd have written you a postcard if I'd known your address.
→ I would have written you a postcard if I had known your address.

Nicht mehr erfüllbare Bedingung im if-Satz: ***past perfect***	Folge im Hauptsatz: *conditional perfect* (**would** + **have** + ***past participle***)
If I had seen Mary,	I would certainly have spoken to her.
Wenn ich Mary gesehen hätte,	hätte ich sie ganz sicher angesprochen.
If you had told me,	I would have done something about it.
Wenn du es mir gesagt hättest,	hätte ich etwas getan.
If you hadn't broken your bike,	you could have ridden it to school.
Wenn du dein Fahrrad nicht kaputt gemacht hättest,	hättest du damit in die Schule fahren können.

Die folgenden Sätze drücken auch nicht mehr erfüllbare Bedingungen aus. Hier wird die Folge aber nicht in der Vergangenheit, sondern in der Gegenwart gedacht:

If you hadn't broken your bike,	you could ride it to school.
Wenn du dein Rad nicht kaputt gemacht hättest,	könntest du damit in die Schule fahren.
If you had bought a new bike,	there wouldn't be any problems.
Wenn du ein neues Rad gekauft hättest,	gäbe es keine Probleme./ würde es keine Probleme geben.

2 What if ...?

Louise is talking to her friend Lisa about the last class trip. They imagine what would have happened if things had gone differently.
Fill in the correct verb forms.

EXAMPLE

If we ______ (know) before that the journey on the bus would be so long, we ______ (not have) such a good time.
If we *had known* before that the journey on the bus would be so long, we *would not have* had such a good time.

1. The bus driver ______ (not shout) at us that it is forbidden to eat on the bus if we ______ (not eat) our sweets.
2. Mrs Robinson ______ (not go) to the police station if she ______ (not find) £10 on the street.
3. If the police ______ (not give) the money back to her, Mrs Robinson ______ (not send) us to the ice cream parlour and she also ______ (not pay) for our ice cream.
4. We ______ (do) much more the next day if the weather ______ (be) better.
5. If we ______ (not stay) so long in our rooms, Mrs Robinson ______ (not get) angry with us because of our untidy rooms.
6. If the boys ______ (not buy) playing cards in the afternoon they ______ (not come) to our room to play with us at night.
7. Mr Davenport ______ (not catch) us if he ______ (not hear) us laughing.
8. If he ______ (not leave) his bed and run into our room, he ______ (not hurt) his leg on one of the bedposts.
9. We ______ (not laugh) so much if he ______ (not fall) right into Paula's arms.
10. It ______ (be) very funny if poor Mr Davenport ______ (not break) his leg.
11. If Mr Davenport ______ (not end up) in hospital we ______ (not return) home so early.

3 Problems in the family

Everyone in Louise's family is having a bad day today. They have been arguing with each other the whole day long. Here is what they were saying.
Decide which one of the two given verb forms is correct. Underline the correct form.

1. Mum: "If you (wouldn't be/weren't) so untidy, Louise, you (found/would find) your things more easily."
2. Louise: "I (didn't have to look/wouldn't have to look) for my things all the time if Joe (didn't go/wouldn't go) into my room and take them all the time."
3. Dad: "I (weren't/wouldn't be) as fat as I am if you (would cook/cooked) healthier things. If it (is/was) my turn to make dinner, I (just cooked/would just cook) vegetables."
4. Mum: "I (didn't buy/wouldn't buy) frozen lasagne if I (would have/had) time to make it myself."
5. Louise: "If mum (wouldn't have/didn't have) to fetch Joe from school, she (had/would have) more time for cooking."
6. Joe: "I (rode/would ride) my bike to school and back if I (was allowed/would be allowed) to."

7. Dad: "If you (would wear/wore) your helmet we (would allow/allowed) you to go to school by bike."
8. Mum: "And if we (wouldn't/didn't) argue so much we (ate/could eat) our dinner now."

4 Lisa's problems are even worse ...

At school, Louise is telling her friend Lisa about all the trouble at home. But Lisa's weekend was even worse.
Translate the following sentences into English. Use the conditional clause type III.

1. Meine Schwestern und ich hätten keine Party gegeben (= to have a party), wenn meine Eltern nicht weggegangen wären.
2. Wenn ich nicht das Kleid meiner Mutter getragen hätte, hätte ich es nicht über und über mit Tomatensoße bekleckert (to get tomato sauce all over it).
3. Mami hätte nicht erfahren (to get to know), dass ich das Kleid ruiniert (to ruin) habe, wenn ich es besser versteckt (to hide) hätte.
4. Wenn sie es nicht gefunden hätte, wäre sie mir nicht so böse gewesen.

GOOD TO KNOW *What to say when you're in the UK*

In diesem Abschnitt des Buches geht es darum, wie man sich in bestimmten Alltagssituationen im englischsprachigen Ausland verhält oder verständigt.

How to give somebody advice – **Wie man jemandem einen Rat gibt**

Willst du einem anderen einen Rat geben, solltest du die folgenden Schritte beachten:

- zuhören und mögliche Fragen klären
- sich möglichst in die Lage des anderen hineinversetzen
- gemeinsames „Brainstorming“, das heißt gemeinsam Ideen zusammentragen oder über Alternativen nachdenken
- ehrlich sein
- verstehen, auch hier notfalls nachfragen

Tipp: Gib keinen Ratschlag, den du nicht auch selbst befolgen würdest!
Beispiel:
If I were in your situation, I would try to tell her how everything happened.
Don't overreact! Try to think first.

Auf der nächsten Seite findest du weitere Redewendungen, die du beim Ratgeben oder beim Bitten um Rat verwenden kannst.

Weitere Redemittel:

I need your advice.	Ich benötige deinen Ratschlag.
to advise somebody	jemanden beraten
I need your help.	Ich benötige deine Hilfe.
Can you help me, please?	Kannst du mir bitte helfen?
Something (has) happened to me.	Mir ist etwas passiert.
Please tell me what happened to you in detail.	Bitte erzähle mir genau, was dir passiert ist.
I didn't understand what you just said.	Ich habe nicht verstanden, was du gerade gesagt hast.
If I were you, I would ...	An deiner Stelle würde ich ...
to take/make a decision	eine Entscheidung treffen
This is difficult.	Dies ist schwierig.
I don't really know what to say.	Ich weiß nicht so recht, was ich sagen soll.
I don't know what advice to give you.	Ich weiß nicht, welchen Rat ich dir geben soll.
I guess/think I would (not) talk to ...	Ich denke, ich würde (nicht) mit ... sprechen

1 Mary's advice

Christine is an exchange student in England. Mary is her host-sister. They get along very well. A misfortune (= Missgeschick) happened to Christine. Now she is asking her host-sister for advice. Sometimes she has problems finding the correct English words. Please help her and fill in the gaps.

1. Mary: Hello, Christine. Good to see you. How are you?
   Christine: I am OK, thank you. But I really ________ (deine Hilfe benötigen). Something ________ just ________ (ist ... passiert). I need ________ (Rat). As I was taking a shower I slipped and broke the soap dish (= Seifenschale). It was ________ (so eine) nice one.
2. Mary: Oh my ... Yes, it was a present from my grandmother a long time ago. My mum loves it.
   Christine: I am ________ (so leidtun). What ________ ________ (können wir tun)?
3. Mary: Well, let's see. – Maybe we can call my grandmother to tell her about what happened. Maybe she will be able to help us.
   Christine: Oh, thank you. ________ (das wäre) great.

GOOD TO KNOW *How to ask for something* – um etwas bitten

Wenn du in einem fremden Land bist, musst du sehr häufig nach etwas fragen oder um etwas bitten. Besonders in England ist es dabei sehr wichtig, höflich zu sein.

Es gibt im Englischen viele unterschiedliche Möglichkeiten, jemanden um etwas zu bitten. Möchte man sich jedoch besonders höflich ausdrücken, verwendet man may oder would. Please wird meistens hinten an die Bitte angehängt und mit einem Komma abgetrennt.

Beispiel:

May I borrow your bike, please?	→ Könnte ich bitte dein Fahrrad leihen?
Would/Could you pass me the butter, please?	→ Könnten Sie mir bitte die Butter reichen?
Would you wait for me, please!	→ Würdest du/Würden Sie bitte auf mich warten!

How to ask for something on the phone

Im Englischen nach Informationen zu fragen, unterscheidet sich nicht grundsätzlich vom Deutschen. Man sollte immer darauf achten, seinen Namen zu nennen und sich möglichst genau auszudrücken. Es kann hilfreich sein, sich vorher Notizen zu machen.

Tipp: Auch hier ist Freundlichkeit gefragt! Verwende wieder Worte wie may und/oder please!

2 Ask someone politely …

1. to drive more slowly.

2. to give you some of that delicious soup.

3. to tell you the way to the railway station.

4. to close the window.

3 Steffi's phone call to the London Youth Hostel

Steffi is planning to go on a trip to London shortly. She is calling the youth hostel in London to get some information. Steffi followed her English teacher's advice to make notes prior to (= vor) the call so that her questions and comments are very precise. Connect the words to make correct sentences.

EXAMPLE

Steffi: I/question./have/a

Die Schrägstriche (/) trennen Wörter, bei den Gedankenstrichen (-) fängt ein neuer Satz an. Weitere Hilfen sind Satzzeichen. Sie verweisen z. B. auf das Ende eines Satzes. Die Großschreibung von Wörtern verweist auf einen Satzanfang.

→ Steffi: *I have a question.*

1. Receptionist:/thank you/Hello,/for calling/the London/Youth Hostel. -
   My name/is/Peter. - may/you/How/I/help?
2. Steffi: Steffi Schneider./my name/Hello,/is/-
   calling/I am/Germany./from -
   some/information. /would like/to get/I -
   a trip/for/one/I am planning/week. -
   how much/I would like/a room/per night./to know/costs -
   how far away/is/from Buckingham Palace./like to know/I would also/the youth hostel/
3. Receptionist: Hello Steffi. vary (= sich unterscheiden) Our rates/for rooms /-
   They depend on (= abhängen von)/the size/of the/room.
4. Steffi: Oh, OK. I see. to stay/girl./I would like/with/another -
   the room/then?/is/How much
5. Receptionist: if you are/per night/is £ 20/staying/The room/in a double room.
6. Steffi: OK, thank you/for/information./this -
   the location?/What/about
7. Receptionist: very/central./We are -
   is/away./ only 10 minutes/Buckingham Palace
8. Steffi: tell me,/on foot/is it/Can you/10 minutes/or by bus?
9. Receptionist: on foot./It's/10 minutes
10. Steffi: wonderful./That/is -
    Can I/phone?/reserve a room/by
11. Receptionist: Yes, of course. - an e-mail./also/You can/send me -
    that/I think/is easier.
12. Steffi: All right. - right away./it/I will send -
    e-mail address?/May I have/your
13. Receptionist: It's peter@londonhostel.com. - writing it/down?/Are you
14. Steffi: Yes, I am. - for/information./the/Thank you/-
    to you/send/I will/shortly./an e-mail - Good bye.
15. Receptionist: your call./and/Good bye/thank you/for

GOOD TO KNOW *How to introduce yourself* – sich vorstellen

Wenn man eine unbekannte Person trifft, stellt man sich zunächst vor. Im Englischen sagt man "How do you do?". Auf diese Frage sollte man jedoch nicht antworten. Dies ist lediglich eine höfliche Art, „Guten Tag" zu sagen.

Manchmal ist es schwierig, in einem Gespräch mit fremden Menschen gleich ein Thema zu finden, über das man reden kann. Trotzdem solltest du auf Fragen niemals nur "Yes" oder "No" antworten. Bei einsilbigen Antworten könnte dein Gegenüber denken, dass du gar nicht an einem Gespräch interessiert bist.
Engländer schütteln sich auch nicht so häufig die Hände wie die Deutschen. Wenn sie jemanden zum ersten Mal treffen oder lange nicht gesehen haben, geben sie sich auch schon einmal die Hand, aber üblich ist es nicht.

Things you can say at the first meeting:

Hello Mr/Mrs [name] ...	Hallo Herr/Frau ...
My name is ... and this is ...	Ich heiße ... und das ist ...
How do you do? I'm pleased to/Nice to meet you!	Guten Tag! Ich freue mich/Schön, Sie kennen zu lernen!
Did you have a nice journey?	Hatten Sie/Hattest du eine gute Reise?
Yes, thank you. It was nice but ...	Ja danke. Sie war gut, jedoch ...
If you would like to (come with me).	Wenn Sie bitte (mit mir kommen) würden.
Thank you. That's very kind of you.	Danke. Das ist sehr nett von Ihnen.

4 When Christine arrived in England ... Track 1

Listen to the following scene on the CD. Then answer the questions below.

Christine from Germany has just arrived at Heathrow Airport in London. Her English host-family, Mr and Mrs Perry and their daughter, Mary, are already waiting for her.

1. How does Mrs Perry introduce herself and her husband?
2. How does Mr Perry greet Christine?
3. And what about Mary? What does she say to greet Christine?
4. What is Christine's answer to Mary?
5. What is Christine's answer when Mrs Perry asks how her journey was?
6. What does Mrs Perry say to show that they want to go to the car?
7. Christine wants to know how long the car ride will take. What is her question?
8. What is Mrs Perry's answer?
9. What does Christine reply when Mr Perry offers to carry her luggage?

GOOD TO KNOW *How to behave at meal times* – beim Essen

Die Briten sagen "Thank you" wenn man ihnen etwas gibt oder als Antwort auf ein Kompliment. Sie sagen "No, thank you", um ein Angebot höflich abzulehnen.
Sie sagen jedoch **niemals** "Please" als Antwort auf "Thank you", wie es in Deutschland üblich ist.
In England sagt man meist nichts als Antwort auf "Thank you". Wenn du jedoch besonders höflich sein möchtest, kannst du "That's alright.", "You're welcome." (= Gern geschehen.), "Don't mention it." (= Nicht der Rede wert.) oder "Not at all." (= Keine Ursache. Gern geschehen.), antworten.
Eine Äußerung wie „Guten Appetit" gibt es im englischsprachigen Raum nicht. Manchmal sagen die Engländer jedoch "Please start." oder "Don't wait for us."
In seltenen Fällen, z. B. wenn sie die deutsche Angewohnheit kennen, hört man auch "Enjoy your meal."

Things you can say at meal times:

Sit down please.	Setz dich doch bitte.
I would like to start with toast.	Ich möchte gerne mit Toast beginnen.
I'd like ..., please.	Ich hätte gerne ... bitte.
Can I have ..., please?	Kann ich bitte ... haben?
Just ... for me, please.	Für mich bitte nur ...
I'd prefer (= vorziehen) ..., please.	Ich würde lieber ... haben, bitte.
Don't go to any trouble, please.	Machen Sie sich bitte keine Umstände.
...if it's no trouble to you.	... wenn es ihnen keine Umstände macht.
That's no trouble at all.	Das ist überhaupt kein Problem.
Can you pass me the ..., please?	Würdest/Könntest du mir ... rübergeben?
Can you give me the ..., please?	Würdest/Könntest du mir ... reichen?
Can I offer you ...?	Darf ich dir/Ihnen ... anbieten?
Help yourself!	Bedien dich! Nimm dir ruhig!
Thank you, I've really had plenty.	Danke, ich bin wirklich satt.
It was delicious.	Es war sehr lecker.
I really enjoyed it.	Es hat mir wirklich gut geschmeckt.
I'm glad you liked it.	Es freut mich, dass es dir geschmeckt hat.
Can I help clear the table?	Kann ich beim Abräumen helfen?
Can I help you with the dishes?	Kann ich beim Abwasch helfen?

5 Christine's first breakfast with the Perrys

Write down Christine's answers. The German sentences help you.

1. Mrs. Perry: Good morning Christine! If you'd like to sit down at the table, I'll prepare breakfast for you and Mary. Would you like to start with orange juice or cornflakes?
   Christine:
   (Christine sagt, dass sie gerne Cornflakes und Orangensaft haben würde, wenn es Mrs Perry keine Umstände macht.)
2. Mrs Perry: That's no trouble at all. Would you prefer a full English breakfast with eggs and bacon or just toast and jam?
   Christine:
   (Christine bittet um Toast und Marmelade für sich. Sie erklärt, dass sie normalerweise morgens nicht sehr viel isst.)
3. Mrs. Perry: And what about you, Mary?
   Mary: Can I have eggs and bacon, please, mum? I'm very hungry today. And I think I'll have juice to start with as well.
   Mrs Perry: Oh, and before I go to the kitchen. Would you two like tea?
   Mary: Yes, please.
   Christine:
   (Christine sagt, dass sie ein Glas Milch vorziehen würde.)
4. Mrs Perry: That's no problem. Well, please start. The toast will be ready in a couple of minutes. And I'll also prepare your bacon and eggs, Mary.
   Christine:
   (Christine bittet Mary, ihr die Butter zu reichen.)
   Mary: Here you are. But be careful, the butter in England is always salted (= gesalzen).

After breakfast:

5. Mrs Perry: Can I offer you anything else, Christine? Some more toast or milk?
   Christine:
   (Christine lehnt höflich ab. Sie erklärt Mrs Perry, dass sie satt ist. Sie sagt auch, dass es sehr lecker war und ihr geschmeckt hat.)
6. Mrs Perry: Thanks Christine. I'm glad you liked it. I hope you'll like dinner as well. We'll have a traditional English dish. Yorkshire pudding with vegetables and gravy. That's a brown sauce. Do you know the dish (= Gericht)?

Christine:

(Christine sagt, dass sie es noch nie gegessen hat, sie es aber schon immer einmal probieren (= try) wollte.)

7. Mrs Perry: Well, we'll see how you like it. And don't worry if you don't like it. We also have some pizza in the freezer.
Christine:

(Christine bedankt sich und fragt, ob sie beim Abwasch helfen kann.)

8. Mrs Perry: Thank you, Christine. That's very kind of you, but it's Mary's turn to wash the dishes today.
Mary: Oh no. Okay mum. I'll do it in a moment. But afterwards I'll show Christine around. We can go shopping in town, if you like?
Christine:

(Christine sagt, dass sie das gerne tun würde. Sie bittet Mary darum, ihr zu zeigen, wo die Bank ist, da sie vorm Einkaufen Geld wechseln (= change money) muss.)
Mary: That's no problem. The bank is on our way!
Mrs Perry: But you mustn't be late for dinner, girls.
Mary: Don't worry, mum. We'll be on time.

GOOD TO KNOW *If one feels ill* – bei Krankheit

Leider kann es vorkommen, dass man sich im Ausland krank fühlt. In diesem Fall sollte man zuerst seine Gastfamilie um Hilfe bitten.

Things you can say if you do not feel well:

I don't fell well today.	Ich fühle mich heute nicht gut.
I've got a bad headache.	Ich habe schreckliche Kopfschmerzen.
... an upset stomach/a stomach ache.	... eine Magenverstimmung/Bauchweh.
... a sore throat/knee. ...	Halsschmerzen/Schmerzen im Knie.
I think I've got flu/a cold.	Ich glaube, ich habe die Grippe/ eine Erkältung.
Would you have any medicine for me?	Haben Sie irgendeine Arznei für mich, bitte?
I've got a terrible cough.	Ich habe schlimmen Husten.
My head hurts.	Mein Kopf tut mir weh.
There's a strange pain in my arm.	Ich habe seltsame Schmerzen im Arm.

6 Christine doesn't feel well.

This morning Christine feels terrible. Write her sentences with the words in brackets.

1. Mrs Perry: Good morning Christine. Oh dear, what's wrong with you. You look very pale (= blass). Aren't you feeling well?
   Christine:
   (no/not much/sleep – think/have/cold)
2. Mrs Perry: Poor girl! Let me feel your temperature. Yes, your forehead (= Stirn) feels a little hot. Do you have a sore throat, too?
   Christine:
   (Yes/throat/hurt – But/stomach/also be/very painful)
3. Mrs Perry: You really should go back to bed. I'll come upstairs with a nice cup of camomile tea for you in a couple of minutes.
   Christine:
   (Thank you. – That/be/nice – Have/any/medicine/me?)

Mrs Perry: I think I have some tablets somewhere. Let me have a look.

One day later:

4. Christine:
   (Good morning – Thanks/medicine/I/feel/better/today – I/just/have/a little cough/no temperature/anymore.)
5. Mrs Perry: I'm very glad that you are feeling better. Maybe we should go to the chemist's later to get you some more medicine for the cough. I suppose you will be fine in a couple of days.

GOOD TO KNOW *At the chemist's*

In England ist der "chemist's" so etwas wie eine Apotheke und ein Drogeriemarkt in einem. Man bekommt dort viele Medikamente auch ohne Rezept vom Arzt.
Schau dir die folgenden Dialoge an.

Beispiele:

Customer: Hello. I'd like something for a sore throat, please.
Chemist: Try these tablets. They're very good!
Customer: Do I need a prescription (= Rezept) for them?
Chemist: No, you don't. Take them three times a day. Do not swallow (= runterschlucken) them. Place a tablet on your tongue and allow it to dissolve (= auf der Zunge zergehen lassen → lutschen).

Customer: Thank you very much. How much is that?
Chemist: That's £ 2.50 altogether then, please.

Chemist: Good morning, how can I help you?
Customer: Good morning. Have you got anything for sunburn (= Sonnenbrand)?
Chemist: Yes, try this cream. Rub it on (= einreiben, auftragen) every morning and evening.
Customer: Thank you very much!

7 At the chemist's

Now write similar dialogues for the following situations. The German sentences in brackets have to be translated.

1. **A headache**

Customer: Excuse me, could you help me, please?
Chemist: Yes, of course. What do you need?
Customer: I've got ______ . Do you have ______ ?
Chemist: Let me see. Do you have a prescription?
Customer: No, ______ (short answer). Is that a problem?
Chemist: Not at all. ______
______
______ at the beginning and no more than ______ a ______ .
(Versuchen Sie diese Tabletten. Sie werden Ihnen helfen. Nehmen Sie am Anfang zwei und nicht mehr als vier am Tag.)
Customer: ______ (Danke). Is there anything else I should do?
Chemist: Yes, ______
______ a lot. Then the tablets will help more quickly.
(Ja, Sie sollten versuchen viel zu trinken.)

2. **A cold**

Customer: ______
______
Chemist: Yes, I have a very good cream. It helps you to breathe (= atmen).
Customer: Thank you. How do I have to use it?
Chemist: ______
______
(Tragen Sie sie dreimal am Tag auf die Brust (= chest) auf. Und sie sollten nicht mehr in die Sonne gehen.)
Customer: ______
Chemist: You're welcome. That's £ 4.75 then, please.

3. **Toothache**

Chemist: Hello,

(Hallo, wie kann ich Ihnen helfen?)

Customer:

(Hallo, ich habe schreckliche Zahnschmerzen. Hätten Sie irgendwelche Medikamente für mich?)

Chemist: ?

(Haben Sie ein Rezept?)

Customer:

(Nein, habe ich nicht. Ist das ein Problem?)

Chemist: Yes, I'm afraid that is a problem. I am not allowed to sell you anything without a prescription. You will have to go to the dentist's first. I'm very sorry about that.

Customer: That's no problem. Thank you for your help. Good bye!

8 Translate this dialogue into German.

A cough

Chemist: Hello, may I help you?

Customer: Yes, please. My little daughter has a terrible cough. I've got a prescription.

Chemist: Let me see. You're lucky, I've got the medicine here. Let me get it for you.

Customer: Thank you very much. Can you tell me how often she has to take it?

Chemist: Yes, how old is your daughter?

Customer: She's three years old.

Chemist: Okay, then you have to give her the medicine three times a day: in the morning after breakfast, in the afternoon and before you put her to bed in the evening. It's a juice, so give her one spoonful. She shouldn't drink anything afterwards.

Customer: Thank you very much for all your help.

Chemist: You're welcome. Good bye. And get well soon, little girl.

Test

1 Adjective or adverb? Tick the correct form.

		A	B
1.	My babysitter is a ... person.	nice	nicely
2.	She speaks very	clear	clearly
3.	Sometimes she has to speak ... to them.	angry	angrily
4.	She is also a ... driver.	safe	safely
5.	She always drives very	slow	slowly
6.	Nothing is ... for her.	impossible	impossibly
7.	Lucy also cooks	good	well
8.	Her meals are very	good	well
9.	Fiona is training ... to be as good as her.	hard	hardly
10.	I am ... lucky to have two such good babysitters.	extreme	extremely
11.	I can also get home ... . No problem.	late	lately
12.	I ... know anyone who is as lucky as we are.	hard	hardly

You get 1 point for each correct answer. **Your points:** ______ /12

2 Tick the correct future form for each sentence.

1. Lucy's mum: "How was your day?"
   Lucy: "Don't ask! Anyway, by the end of next year I ______ school."
   A will finish B will have finished C finishes

2. Lucy: "I ______ my career counsellor next week to talk about my future."
   A will have met B meet C am meeting

3. Lucy's mum: "You still don't know what you want to do? How many times have I ..."
   Lucy: "I have to hurry, mum! My bus ______ in ten minutes."
   A will have left B is going to leave C leaves

4. Lucy's mum: "Where are you going? You just came back from school!"
   Lucy: "I ______ at Mrs Alexander's house at 4 o'clock."
   A am babysitting B will have babysitted C babysit

5. Lucy: "And yes, mum, I ______ my homework after the babysitting."
   A do B will have done C will do

6. Lucy's mum: "You are working too much, Lucy!"
   Lucy: "I know! By the time I go to bed I ______ for more than eight hours. But I really need the money."
   A will work B will have been working C am working

7. Lucy [to herself]: "It looks as if it ______. Maybe I should take an umbrella!"
   A ☐ is going to rain B ☐ will have rained C ☐ will be raining

8. Lucy's mum: "Lucy, it's your turn to clean the dishes today! When are you ..."
   Lucy: "I ______ late if I don't hurry up now, mum. Bye!"
   A ☐ am being B ☐ will be C ☐ will have been

You get 1 point for each correct answer. **Your points:** ______ /8

3 Fill in the correct passive voice. Be careful with the tenses.

1. The Tower of London ______ (visit) by many tourists from all over the world.
2. Over the centuries it ______ (put hier: verwenden) to many different purposes.
3. For a long time it ______ (use = nutzen) as a prison.
4. But it ______ (never/use) as a church.
5. When it was a prison, its captives ______ (not treat) well.
6. Sometimes they ______ even ______ (not give) food.
7. Today, the "Bloody Tower" ______ (show) to tourists on guided tours.
8. It's the place where the prisoners ______ (keep) in the past.
9. Some of the instruments of torture ______ (can/still/see) there.
10. If you haven't been there yet, don't worry. I guess they ______ ______ (display = ausstellen) for many more years to come.

You get 1 point for each correct answer. **Your points:** ______ /10

4 Tick the correct reflexive proverb.

	A	B
1. Mrs Alexander: "Tony told me he painted it ...?"	☐ him	☐ himself
2. Tony told Lucy a story, but she didn't believe ...	☐ him	☐ himself
3. Mrs Alexander: "You mustn't pay for ... ."	☐ me	☐ myself
4. Mrs Alexander: "I want to pay for ... ."	☐ me	☐ myself
5. Lucy: "How can these people call ... teachers?"	☐ them	☐ themselves
6. These symbols – what do people call ... ? – Icons?	☐ them	☐ themselves
7. Lucy's mum: "Oh Lucy, why can't you decide ... ?"	☐ –	☐ yourself
8. The kids told ... funny stories.	☐ each other	☐ them
9. Lucy: "So we ... again next Thursday?"	☐ meet	☐ meet us
10. Fiona: "Lucy and I have known ... for years."	☐ each other	☐ us

11. Lucy: “Mum always worries ... when I’m out late.” ☐ herself ☐ –

You get 1 point for each correct answer. **Your points:** ____ /11

5 Read the sentences. Then decide which conditional clause it is.

1. If Grandma was younger, she would travel more.
   → Type ____
2. If Grandma and Grandad had never met, my father would not exist.
   → Type ____
3. If Grandma comes tomorrow, we will go to the cinema.
   → Type ____
4. If my Grandad had been alive on Grandma’s birthday, she would have been happier.
   → Type ____
5. If I have grandchildren, I will also be nice to them.
   → Type ____

You get 1 point for each correct answer. **Your points:** ____ /5

6 Just for fun. A quiz on British customs and manners (= Manieren).
Write down: True or false. Correct the false statements.

1. If you ask for something in Britain, you should use the word “please” as often as you can. Even small children are taught this “magic word” when they learn to talk.
2. If somebody says to you, “How do you do?” he or she wants to hear how you feel or if you have any problems. You can tell them about your bad mood or that you have a terrible headache and need to go to the doctor’s.
3. Don’t forget to say “Please” after someone says “Thank you” to you.
4. The British never shake hands, except when they meet Germans.
5. The British think it is rude (= unhöflich) if you just say “Yes” or “No” when they offer you something.

6. If somebody offers you something you don't like, it is polite to say "No, thank you."

7. If you are staying with a British family you should never start eating before your host-mother or host-father has said "Mealtime" or "Good appetite".

You get 1 point for each correct answer. **Your points:** /7

7 Say it in English.

1. Was sagst du, nachdem dir jemand vorgestellt wurde?

2. Was sagst du, wenn du jemandem deinen Freund/deine Freundin vorstellen möchtest?

3. Wie fragst du, wo die nächste Bushaltestelle ist?

4. Wie sagst du, dass du etwas nicht verstanden hast und die Person bittest, es zu wiederholen?

5. Wie bittest du jemanden darum, dir einen Rat zu geben?

6. Wie sagst du, dass du lieber Toast zum Frühstück essen möchtest?

7. Wie bittest du jemanden am Tisch darum, dir die Butter zu reichen?

8. Wie sagst du, dass dir das Essen geschmeckt hat?

You get 1 point for each correct answer. **Your points:** /8

8 Some people ask you for help. How do you react? Tick the polite answer.

1. Excuse me.

A ☐ What do you want?
B ☐ How can I help you?
C ☐ Huh?

2. Could you help me please?
   - A ☐ No. I don't want to.
   - B ☐ I only help nice people.
   - C ☐ I'd be glad to help you.

3. Could you tell me the way to the bank?
   - A ☐ Yes, of course. It's just over there.
   - B ☐ Why don't you buy a map?
   - C ☐ It's more fun if you look yourself.

4. I'm sorry, I can't find your CD!
   - A ☐ Well, let's look for it together.
   - B ☐ Can't you do *anything* right?
   - C ☐ I'll never give you a CD again.

5. Thanks for all your help.
   - A ☐ What help?
   - B ☐ You're welcome!
   - C ☐ Forget it.

6. Can you pass me the juice, please?
   - A ☐ It's nearly empty. I'll have the rest.
   - B ☐ It's empty. I'll get you some more.
   - C ☐ It's empty. There's more in the fridge.

You get 1 point for each correct answer. **Your points:** ______ /6

9 Mediation: Alistair is ill

Your exchange partner Alistair is staying with you in Germany at the moment, but he is ill. His German is not very good and the people around you do not speak English very well. You have to translate.

1. Mutter: Alistair, geht es dir gut? Du siehst so blass aus.
   You: Alistair, my mother asks if you ______________________.
   She says ______________________

2. Alistair: Well, I didn't sleep very much last night. I've had a terrible stomach ache. It's better now, but I still feel dizzy (= schwindelig).
   You: Er sagt, er habe ______________________
   ____
   ____

3. Mutter: Deine Stirn ist ja ganz heiß, Alistair. Ich glaube, du hast Fieber.
   You: My mum says ______________________
   ____

4. Alistair: Maybe she's right. I also have a sore throat. Do you think she might have some medicine for me?
   You: ______________________
   ____
   ____

5. Mutter: Lass mich mal nachsehen. Nein, ich habe keine Medizin mehr. Ich glaube, wir sollten besser mit ihm zum Arzt gehen.
You:

6. Alistair: Thank you, but I don't think that's necessary. My mother always gives me hot milk and honey if I have a sore throat. Do you think your mum would be so kind as to make me one?
You:

7. Mutter: Ja natürlich, das ist kein Problem. Ich werde ihm gleich eine machen. Er sollte aber besser wieder ins Bett gehen und ein wenig schlafen. Dann wird es ihm morgen sicher wieder besser gehen.
You:

You get 2 points for each correct answer. **Your points:** /14

10 Match the English sentences with the correct German translation. Put in the right letter

1. ☐ Do you feel a pain in your leg when you move it?
2. ☐ Rub the cream on every morning and evening.
3. ☐ Take this prescription to the chemist's.
4. ☐ I've got a headache.
5. ☐ I've got flu.
6. ☐ When did the pain start?
7. ☐ What can I do for you?
8. ☐ Is there anything I can do for you?
9. ☐ I've got a sore throat.
10. ☐ I've got a terrible cough.
11. ☐ Rub the cream on twice a day.
12. ☐ I've got sunburn.
13. ☐ You have to take the tablets three times a day.
14. ☐ I've got stomach ache.

A Ich habe Kopfschmerzen.
B Ich habe Bauchschmerzen.
C Ich habe einen Sonnenbrand.
D Ich habe einen schrecklichen Husten.
E Nehmen Sie dieses Rezept mit zur Apotheke.
F Kann ich irgendetwas für Sie tun?
G Sie müssen die Tabletten dreimal am Tag nehmen.
H Fühlen Sie einen Schmerz im Bein, wenn Sie es bewegen?
I Tragen Sie die Salbe jeden Morgen und Abend auf.
J Ich habe die Grippe.
K Was kann ich für Sie tun?
L Wann haben die Schmerzen angefangen?
M Tragen Sie die Creme zweimal täglich auf.
N Ich habe Halsschmerzen.

You get 1 point for each correct answer. **Your points:** ____ /14

Your total points out of 95 points: ____

- More than 80? Very good.
- More than 70? Good.
- Less than 47? Have a look at the grammar and mediation pages again. You CAN do better.

3 Texte verstehen

Das solltest du am Ende der Klasse 7 können:

im Bereich Lesen und verstehen:

▷ Wortbedeutungen aus dem Zusammenhang erschließen und dir Notizen machen

im Bereich Hören und verstehen:

▷ Längere, anspruchsvollere Texte verstehen, die in annähernd normalem Sprechtempo vorgetragen werden

▷ Dabei Gliederungsprinzipien anwenden, um einfache Sachverhalte wiederzugeben

3.1 Lesen und verstehen

GOOD TO KNOW *Fictional texts*

Du solltest nach dem Lesen einer Geschichte ihren Inhalt wiedergeben und die wichtigsten Personen nennen können. Notizen können dir dabei helfen.

So kannst du eine Geschichte besser verstehen:

1. *Read for gist*	Beim ersten Lesen konzentrierst du dich auf die Hauptgeschichte eines Textes und die Personen, die darin vorkommen. Es geht um die Antworten auf die Fragen: Who? What? When? Where? Why? Kleinere Details und unbekannte Wörter solltest du erst einmal ignorieren.
2. *Read for detail*	Lies die Geschichte erneut. Gliedere sie in Sinnabschnitte und finde für jeden Sinnabschnitt eine Überschrift.
3. *Intelligent guessing*	Wenn in einem Abschnitt ein Wort vorkommt, das du nicht kennst, überlege, bevor du es nachschlägst. Kannst du den Abschnitt auch verstehen, wenn du das Wort nicht kennst? Dann musst du es auch nicht nachschlagen!
4. *Make notes*	Mach dir Notizen, damit du nichts vergisst. Es ist eine gute Idee, kleine Überschriften für deine Abschnitte zu finden. Dann kannst du für jeden Abschnitt mit deinen eigenen Worten notieren, was in ihm passiert.

Mit der folgenden Geschichte bekommst du ein Beispiel für die Arbeit mit Texten. Lies die Geschichte und wende die einzelnen Schritte genau an. Löse danach die Aufgaben. Du kannst dir den Text auch auf der CD anhören.

Wenn du über einen Text schreibst, verwendest du immer das *simple present*, denn der Inhalt bleibt immer der gleiche, gleichgültig, wie oft oder wann du den Text liest.

Dinge, die zeitlich vor der eigentlichen Geschichte liegen, kannst du im *simple past* beschreiben.

Tipp: Um herauszufinden, ob du alle wichtigen Punkte eines Textes verstanden hast, kannst du zu jedem Text auch selbst Fragen finden und dann die Antworten darauf geben.

Sir Francis Drake's Plan

Track 2

1 **First read the text for gist.**
You can also listen to the text on the CD.

It was a nice, calm evening and still very hot at Plymouth harbour. The English fleet had been lying there at anchor for many weeks. The sailors were counting the days in that quiet July of 1588. Nearly every boy and girl in England had heard by now that the Spaniards were ready to attack the English with the most enormous fleet anyone had ever seen.
People said that the Spanish called it the Great Armada. Spain, with its Catholic king, was the strongest and richest country in Europe at that time. Queen Elizabeth I, who was a Protestant, wanted to be stronger and richer than the Spanish. She had given orders to build lots of ships. One of her most talented captains, Sir Francis Drake, had attacked Spanish towns and ships with the help of many other English ships and had stolen their treasures for his queen. The English sailors knew that the Spaniards would come with their legendary ships to fight them, or even to destroy them. They wanted revenge for the terrible deeds of Sir Francis and his men. The question everyone talked about was: When would they come?
There were guards in the several lookouts whose only job was to search for a ship on the horizon, while the captains enjoyed the free time. During the first couple of days everybody had been glad about some free minutes to take a rest. But after all these weeks they were bored and there was not much else to do than play a game of cards or play bowls on the grass behind the church. Sir Francis Drake, the captain of one of the biggest ships of the English fleet, took the time to write his daily entry into his logbook. He seemed to be enjoying the quiet days, but inside he felt this restlessness he always had before going on

his ship again. His home was the sea, his best friend his ship. He looked up from his logbook and took a look around him.

Something was different that warm evening in July. Many of the sailors seemed to be in a very bad mood. They were sweating and restless. Some of them had started to fight about their game of cards when suddenly the shouts of men could be heard in the harbour: "The Spaniards, they're coming!" "Get ready! We saw over a hundred ships in the Channel!" Surely, the English Channel was very big and it would take the Spaniards some more minutes, maybe hours until they arrived at Plymouth, but the cries of the men from the lookout had just finished when everybody started to panic. Sailors were running to their ships, officers were shouting for their men and the commander of the fleet, Lord Howard, ordered everybody to their ships. "There is no time to lose," he said, when he suddenly realized that Sir Francis Drake was still writing in his logbook.

He didn't look as if he wanted to go to his ship. Lord Howard was very puzzled. "Didn't you hear my order, Sir Francis?" "Yes, I did," Drake answered, "but I don't think we will be able to beat them if we start the battle now. I have a better plan." Soon all the men knew what they had to do. Lord Howard had not been fully convinced by Drake's plan, but it was worth a try. It would not be easy to defeat the Spaniards with all their ships anyway, so why not do something they would never expect? Later, Howard's men left Plymouth harbour to do what Drake had told them. The plan was to follow the Great Armada and to attack them from behind. The plan was good, but when the men saw the ships their hearts sank. There must have been about 130 ships, each much bigger than their own ones.

The good thing about small ships is that they can sail much faster, so they soon reached the Spanish ships and started to fire cannonballs at them. Afterwards the English ships turned away quickly before the Spanish could fire and hit back. After some time, the English still at their tail shooting at them, the Spaniards reached the harbour of Calais, on the French coast. Everyone knew that it was nearly impossible to attack them there, but again Sir Francis had an idea.

Some of the oldest ships were filled with pitch and tar and in the night set on fire. With the help of other ships the English let them drift towards the Spanish fleet in the harbour. A lot of the Spanish ships caught fire quickly. The night was bright with the light from the fires and there were shouts of terrified Spanish sailors everywhere. They tried to rescue the rest of their ships by sailing away from the fires, so it was easy for the English to surround them and sink some of the biggest Spanish ships. The rest of them sailed away, out into the dark North Sea.

Long after this big battle it was said that only 54 out of the 130 ships returned to Spain, after some more ships had been lost on the way back in a heavy storm off the coasts of Ireland and Scotland.

2 **Complete the notes.**

Write short answers to the questions.

Who? → Sir Francis Drake, Lord ____________, ____________ and ____________ sailors, the Great ____________, an English ____________

What? → ____________

When? → ____________

Where? → ____________

Why? → ____________

3 **Now read the text for detail. Find headings for the following sections.**

EXAMPLE

lines 1 – 5 → *The tension at Plymouth harbour* (introduction)

lines 6 – 14 → ____________

lines 15 – 23 → ____________

lines 24 – 33 → ____________

lines 34 – 48 → ____________

lines 49 – 55 → ____________ (climax)

lines 56 – 58 → ____________ (ending)

4 **Read/listen to the text again and answer the following questions in your exercise book.**

1. Where does the English fleet wait?
2. Why do the Spaniards want to attack the English?
3. What happens after the sailor in the lookout shouts that the Spaniards are coming?
4. What does Lord Howard mean when he says “There’s no time to lose” (l. 32)?
5. Why is Lord Howard so puzzled when he sees Sir Francis Drake writing into his logbook as all the other sailors are running to their ships?
6. Why does Sir Francis Drake not run to his ship like all the other men?
7. What is Sir Francis Drake’s plan?
8. What is the advantage (= Vorteil) of small ships and how does that help the English?
9. Where does the Great Armada retreat to (= sich zurückziehen) after the first fight?
10. What are fire-ships and what do the English do with them?

GOOD TO KNOW *Intelligent guessing: new words*

Manche Wörter kannst du dir von deutschen oder schon bekannten englischen Wörtern ableiten.
Beispiele: anchor – Anker lookout – Ausguck

Andere Wörter kannst du erschließen, wenn du dir den ganzen Abschnitt ansiehst.
Beispiele: fleet: sailors (Zeile 4) und harbour (Zeile 1) lassen erkennen, dass es etwas mit der Schifffahrt zu tun haben muss. In Zeile 12 ist von „legendary ships" die Rede, fleet muss also „viele Schiffe" bedeuten, also „Flotte".
Wörter wie pitch (Pech) und tar (Teer) musst du nachschlagen, um herauszufinden, was sie bedeuten. Du kannst aber auch ohne Nachschlagen verstehen, dass es Materialien sein müssen, die das Schiff besser brennen lassen. Zum Textverständnis ist es also nicht so wichtig, die genaue Bedeutung zu kennen.

5 Find the meaning of the following words from the text.
Follow the examples above.

1. horizon – ____________
2. commander – ____________
3. play bowls – ____________
4. logbook – ____________
5. cannonball – ____________
6. drift – ____________
7. revenge (**Tipp:** Vielleicht kannst du es aus dem 2. Abschnitt erraten.) – ____________
8. deeds – ____________
9. take a rest – ____________
10. restless – ____________
11. at their tail – ____________

REMEMBER *Past perfect*

In Sir Francis Drakes Geschichte begegnet dir oft das *past perfect*, z. B. had heard (Zeile 4).
Das *past perfect* drückt Vorzeitigkeit aus. Man gebraucht es für Handlungen, die vor einer anderen Handlung der Vergangenheit stattgefunden haben (Plusquamperfekt).

Um zu berichten, was in der Vergangenheit passierte, benutzt du zunächst das *simple past* oder das *past progressive*.
Beispiele: Sarah arrived at the party. (*simple past*)
Sarah was standing at the bus stop when … (*past progressive*)
Diese Sätze könnten der Anfangspunkt einer Geschichte sein. Er liegt in der Vergangenheit.
Willst du über etwas berichten, was passiert ist, bevor Sarah auf die Party bzw. zur Bushaltestelle kam, benutzt du das *past perfect*. Das *past perfect* wird mit had + *past participle* gebildet.
Beispiele: When Sarah arrived at the party, Peter **had** already **gone** home.
Sarah was standing at the bus stop. She **had finished** her shopping. Then …

Hier ist eine Übersicht:

Vorvergangenheit	Vergangenheit	Gegenwart
Peter had gone home.	Sarah arrived.	I'm telling the story.
Sarah had been shopping.	Sarah waited for the bus.	I'm telling the story.

6 Simple past or past perfect? Put in the missing verb forms (simple or progressive form).

Sir Francis Drake is back in London after the battle and tells his story.

1. Everything ______ (be) quiet for days, but that evening the Spanish ships were seen.
2. It ______ (be) one of these quiet evenings in the harbour when all the boys ______ (rest) and ______ (play) cards.
3. There ______ (be) a rumour for days that the Spanish would come, but nothing ______ (can be) seen.
4. Suddenly there ______ (be) shouts everywhere and Lord Howard ______ (order) the men to their ships.
5. He ______ (be) very calm before, but that evening he ______ (lose) his head. However, things ______ (go) well after I ______ (tell) him my plan.
6. We ______ (attack) the Spaniards from behind until they ______ (reach) the harbour of Calais.

7. Up to then the French ______________ (always be) very friendly to the Spanish.
8. My second plan, to set their ships on fire, ______________ (work) very well. They ______________ (not expect) anything like that and ______________ (not leave) the harbour. That ______________ (be) their mistake and our victory.

7 Translate these sentences into English. Use the past perfect where possible.

Peter is a member of his school's drama group. This year they want to play the story of Sir Francis Drake and the Great Armada.

1. Als Peter ankam, waren die meisten Rollen (= most of the parts) bereits von seinen Klassenkameraden besetzt worden (= take).
2. Peter hatte Sir Francis Drake spielen wollen, aber es war nur noch die Rolle eines Matrosen (= sailor) übrig (= left), als er mit seinem Lehrer sprach.
3. Nach einiger Zeit war Peter sehr zufrieden (= satisfied) mit seiner Rolle, da sie ihm die Zeit gab, auch am Bühnenbild (= stage set) zu arbeiten.
4. Er hatte das große Schiff fast fertiggestellt, als der Unfall passierte.
5. Stewart, der Sir Francis Drake spielte und Peter in seiner Freizeit mit dem Schiff geholfen hatte, fiel von einer Leiter und brach sich das Bein.
6. Bislang (= so far) hatte alles gut funktioniert (= work well) in der Theatergruppe, aber nun gab es (= there be) ein Chaos. Einige Schüler schrien (= scream) und andere riefen den Lehrer.
7. Als der Krankenwagen (= ambulance) ankam, hatten sich alle (= everyone) bereits wieder beruhigt (= calm down again). Stewart wurde ins Krankenhaus gebracht (= take to hospital).
8. Es war gut, dass Peter Stewarts Rolle auch gelernt hatte, denn nun stellte sich heraus (= turn out), dass Stewart Sir Francis Drake nicht mit einem Gipsbein (= with his leg in plaster) spielen konnte.
9. Als der Abend der Vorstellung (= performance) kam, war Peter sehr nervös. Er fühlte sich, als könne er sich an kein einziges Wort seines Textes erinnern (= not remember any word of).
10. Aber als er die Bühne (= stage) zum ersten Mal betrat (= enter), gab es eine große Überraschung (= surprise). Stewart war von seinen Eltern zur Vorstellung gebracht worden. Er saß in der ersten Reihe (= row) mit einem großem Schild (= sign) in seinen Händen, das sagte „Peter, du kannst es!“ (= you can do it).
11. Das Stück (= play) war ein großer Erfolg (= success). Als das Publikum (= audience) applaudierte (= cheer), konnte sich Peter nicht mehr daran erinnern, warum er zuvor so nervös gewesen war.

Like a spider in a cave

Track 3

1 Read the text.

The men were angry and impatient. They had been in this dirty old cave for over two months now. They had been waiting but nothing had happened. When they first came to the cave they had all been very happy to have found such a good hiding place. The cave was quite big, enough room for the 36 men and their king, Robert the Bruce of Scotland. "If we put some more rocks in front of the cave, King Edward and his men will never find us," Robert the Bruce said after they had found the cave.

Scotland was at war. King Robert wanted a free and independent Scotland, but his enemy, King Edward, wanted to rule over both England and Scotland, so he had brought a big army to fight against the rebels. The Scottish army had lost almost every battle. Robert the Bruce just did not have enough men to beat the English soldiers. He needed time to think of a good strategy before the next battle, so he had decided to make the cave the new home for himself and his men.

King Robert could feel that his men were restless. They wanted to fight against the people they hated so much because they had taken away their land, made them prisoners and even killed their people. "The men are soldiers, Robert, they would rather die than hide here any longer," Walter the Steward, Robert's good friend, said. "They will have to be patient," King Robert replied. "We have fought and lost so many battles, we must win the next one. If only I had more men. I can't fight another battle with only a few men." "And you can't win a battle in a cave, can you?" Sir Andrew Douglas shouted at his king. He was a very good soldier, but also sometimes wild and hot-headed. "I won't hide any longer," he shouted, ran out of the cave, took his horse and rode away angrily. "Another good man has left you," Walter said with a sad voice. "If you don't do something soon, there will be more to follow him." The King looked very sad and said: "I wish I knew what to do."

Later that evening Robert was watching the fire in the cave, still thinking about his problem. He couldn't sleep, he was too worried. His men were thin and weak, they didn't have enough food anymore. At dinner Walter had even shared the little food he had with the other men. He was such a kind man. King Robert had not eaten anything. He had just not been able to. He had thought of his dead brothers and the rest of his family, prisoners of the English, even his wife and children.

At least his men could sleep. It was silent in the cave. Lost in his thoughts he watched a small spider which was spinning a web in a corner of the cave. Because of the wind and the rough rocks the web broke again and again, but the spider did not give up. One - two - three times it started again. While he was watching it, Robert suddenly felt very tired and fell asleep.

When he woke up again it was already morning. He opened his eyes and looked around. All his men were still sleeping. He looked in the direction where he had seen the spider in the night. King Robert smiled for the first time in many days. In front of him was a perfect spider's web. "It never gave up," he said to himself. "The spider lost its web again and again, but it always started again." He looked at the web for a long time. "I can do it like the spider. I will not give up! If that little spider can finish its web, I can beat the English." Suddenly he felt strong again.

He made up his plan and woke his men up. "Walter, send a soldier to Stirling. Tell them that we will arrive in four days, that we are ready for the next battle and that we need every man. I'm sure they will help us." It was in the year 1314 that Robert the Bruce fought the battle that was to free Scotland from the English. Today it is famous as the Battle of Bannockburn. 9,000 brave Scotsmen faced 25,000 English soldiers - and won! Their King had told them that the enemy would be defeated if they just didn't give up.

2 Work on the following questions and tasks.

1. Who?
2. What?
3. When?
4. Where?
5. Why?
6. Find headings for each paragraph and note them in the prepared lines in the text.
7. Write down the words you do not know and explain their meaning.
8. Why are King Robert's men angry and thin?
9. How does the spider help Robert the Bruce?
10. What kind of person is Walter the Steward?
11. What do Robert's men do to hide from King Edward and his men?
12. Describe Sir Andrew Douglas and why he shouts at King Robert.
13. Why was the Battle of Bannockburn such a spectacular battle?

3 Translate the sentences into English. Use the past perfect where possible.

1. Robert the Bruce und seine Männer verließen die Höhle. Sie hatten dort viele Monate lang gewohnt.
2. Die Menschen aus Stirling hatten gehört, dass König Robert Hilfe brauchte, also kamen sie alle, um mit ihm zu kämpfen.
3. Sogar Sir Andrew, der von der Höhle weggerannt war, kam zurück, um seinem König zu helfen.
4. Obwohl sie die Schotten so oft besiegt hatten, verloren die Engländer die Schlacht von Bannockburn.
5. Robert vergaß die Spinne nie, die ihm in der Höhle die Augen geöffnet hatte.

GOOD TO KNOW *Factual texts* – **Sachtexte**

Sachtexte begegnen dir häufig, wenn du etwas nachforschst, zum Beispiel bei der Arbeit an einem Projekt für die Schule. Sachtexte findet man in Broschüren, auf Internetseiten, in Zeitungen und Zeitschriften usw.
Beim Lesen von Sachtexten geht es besonders darum, schnell und sicher die Informationen im Text zu finden, die wichtig sind.
Aber Vorsicht: Den Inhalten von Sachtexten, besonders, wenn man sie im Internet findet, sollte man nie blind vertrauen! Überprüfe die Informationen anhand weiterer Quellen, wenn es möglich ist.

So filterst du aus einem Sachtext wichtige Informationen heraus:

1. *Skimming*	Mit dieser Technik findest du heraus, ob der Text für deine Zwecke hilfreich oder interessant ist. Schau den Text rasch durch, ohne jedes Wort zu lesen. Suche nach Schlagworten, wie z. B. nach Nomen und Adjektiven, die für dein Thema relevant sind. Nun kannst du in wenigen Sätzen sagen, wovon der Text handelt.
2. *Scanning*	In diesem zweiten Schritt solltest du dir erst die Themen herausschreiben, für die du nach Informationen suchst. Dann lässt du deine Augen Zeile für Zeile über den Text schweifen – wieder ohne jedes Wort zu lesen. Markiere dir am Rand mit einem Bleistift die Passagen, die für dich wichtig sind.
3. *Intelligent guessing*	Gibt es in dem Text Wörter, die du unbedingt wissen musst, um den Text verstehen oder erklären zu können? Versuche, sie von dir bekannten englischen oder deutschen Wörtern abzuleiten, bevor du sie nachschlägst.
4. *Make notes*	Deine Notizen sollten nach deinen Themen geordnet sein. Das jeweilige Thema ist die Überschrift, darunter notierst du dir alle Informationen aus dem Text. So hast du gleich eine Gliederung für eine Textzusammenfassung.

1 Skim the following text. Look through the text quickly.

Mark the keywords, the first ones have already been done for you. These keywords are underlined. Then write down in one or two sentences what the text is about.

Oxford

Track 4

If you follow the River Thames from London to the west of the country you will after approximately 60 miles reach one of the most <u>beautiful old towns</u> in England, <u>Oxford</u>. The Norman Robert d'Oilly conquered Oxford in 1066, but it was only a little village at that time. Its <u>name</u> is even older than the town itself. For centuries the Saxon farmers and their oxen had crossed the river here at the ford, a shallow place where it was possible to walk across the Thames. That's where the name comes from: Oxen-ford. Robert quickly reinforced the town wall and built a stone bridge across the River Thames, as well as a castle with a chapel.

The priests of the chapel, the canons, were soon known for their knowledge and in 1100 the first lecture was held. This was the start of Oxford University. In the year 1216 the university already counted more than 1000 masters and students.

A student started his studies at the age of sixteen in those days. Only boys were allowed to study. For seven years they had to learn everything about grammar, logic, rhetoric - to be able to speak and think clearly - arithmetic, geometry, astronomy, music and philosophy. After these seven years the student had an examination in which he had to prove his knowledge before he could leave the university, a master himself.

The number of students grew quickly and they all needed a place to live and to be taught. Many new buildings were erected; each master had to take care of the students in his hall, as the houses were called. This is why even today there is not really just one university in Oxford. Oxford University is more a collection of many small colleges, which still form the centre of the town.

Though girls were finally allowed to study at a special girls' college in 1878, they couldn't get a degree until 1921. Since 1979 nearly every college in Oxford has had to let girls in, though in 1974 only five of the originally boys-only colleges admitted girls.

The 22 colleges are still the main source of income. Not only jobs as teachers are offered in Oxford, you also need lots of people to look after the houses, gardens, the more than 11,000 students, shops, pubs, cinemas, libraries and so on.

There are also lots of jobs in the William Morris car factory on the outskirts of the town, which was founded in the 1920s.

Nowadays Oxford is a great place for shopping, too. You will find all the shops, both big and small, around the High Street. You can also visit one of the many museums or tour the College buildings. And you shouldn't miss going on a tour on the river in one of the famous boats, the punts, or in a rowing boat.

2 Scan the text.

Look at the text again, but do not read every word. Is there any information about these topics? Tick (✔).

	yes	no
1. famous people		
2. industry		
3. going to London		
4. history		
5. free time activities		
6. spending money		
7. scary situations		
8. the royal family		

3 Complete the list of topics from the text.

- jobs (pubs, shops, ...)
- leisure (rowing, ...)
- ...

GOOD TO KNOW *Word families*

Man kann neue Wörter oft erschließen, wenn man ein Nomen, Verb oder Adjektiv kennt, das aus der gleichen Wortfamilie stammt.
Wenn du z. B. weißt, dass ein freezer ein Gefrierschrank ist, kannst du erraten, dass das Verb to freeze „gefrieren, frieren" heißt.

In vielen englischen Wortfamilien wird aus einem Verb ein Nomen gebildet, indem man an den Infinitiv -er anhängt.
Beispiel: speak → a speaker (= Sprecher).

Man kann auch aus Verben oder Nomen Adjektive formen, indem man z. B. ein -ful anhängt.
Beispiel: delight (= Freude, Entzücken) → delightful (= entzückend, wunderbar)

Bildet man aus einem Adjektiv ein Nomen, so geschieht das sehr häufig durch das Anhängen von -ness. Dies entspricht dem deutschen -heit.
Beispiel: wild → wildness (Wildheit)
Achtung: „Wildnis" heißt auf Englisch wilderness.

Endet ein Adjektiv auf y, so wird daraus beim Anhängen von -ness ein i.
Beispiel: lazy → laziness (Faulheit)

4 Find the words.

Find the nouns to the verbs in italics (= kursiv gedruckt).

1. Anna likes to *dance* to music. If she takes lessons she will be a good ______ soon.
2. Thomas *caught* the most difficult ball in the last baseball match. He is an excellent ______.
3. Who is that on the poster? – That's my favourite ______. Do you want to hear how he sounds when he *sings*?
4. Oh, this is a very modern ______. Do you often *cook* on it?
5. Van Gogh is a very famous ______. He *painted* lots of pictures in his life.
6. Tommy didn't want to *eat* today. – Really? Normally he is a good ______!
7. My sister is learning to *drive* at the moment. Mum says she will be a very careful ______.
8. Look how Pete *rides* his horse. I don't know any better ______ than him.

5 Try to translate the words into German.

1. helpful → German: ______
2. safety → German: ______
3. non-smoker → German: ______
4. anger → German: ______
5. earliness → German: ______
6. bitterness → German: ______
7. shoemaker → German: ______
8. wonderful → German: ______
9. building → German: ______

6 Form the nouns to the adjectives below and translate them into German.

	adjective	noun		German
1.	helpful –		=	
2.	helpless –		=	
3.	careless –		=	
4.	early –		=	
5.	wet –		=	
6.	ready –		=	
7.	strange –		=	
8.	lonely –		=	

REMEMBER Modale Hilfsverben

would, shall, should

Im Englischen stehen die modalen Hilfsverben immer zusammen mit einem Vollverb im Infinitiv. Mit would kannst du um etwas bitten oder ausdrücken, dass du gern etwas tun würdest.

Du gebrauchst should, wenn du jemandem etwas dringend raten oder empfehlen möchtest.

Mit shall kannst du Vorschläge machen oder um Rat bitten.

Beispiele: I **would** do the shopping later when the shops are emptier if I were you.
Would you please help me with the shopping bags?
You **shouldn't** buy so many sweets. They are unhealthy.
What **shall** we eat instead of sweets? **Shall** we buy sweet fruit?

Stacy from the USA visits Oxford

Stacy, a girl from the USA, is reading a novel about a young girl who wanted to study in Oxford in 1900. She likes the book very much and wants to spend her summer holidays in Oxford. She wants to go to summer school, a programme for young students who want to see what studying is like and can study for 4-8 weeks in the summer, when all the real students are on holiday. She wants to know what else she can do in her free time and she is also very interested in the history of Oxford. She writes a letter to the tourist information centre to find out more.

GOOD TO KNOW *Writing letters* – Briefe schreiben

Briefe beginnst du immer mit "Dear ..." und dem Namen der Person, an die du schreibst, bzw. "Dear Sir or Madam", wenn du keinen Namen kennst und nicht weißt, ob es ein Mann oder eine Frau ist, an den oder die du schreibst.

Du endest mit "Yours" bei inoffiziellen Briefen, mit "Yours sincerely" bei förmlichen Briefen und mit "Love" bei Freunden. Darunter schreibst du jeweils deinen Namen.

1 Write a letter to Stacy.

You work for the tourist information centre. Give Stacy the information she asked for. Use *would, shall, should* and your notes from exercise 3 (p. 63). Do not copy the text.

GOOD TO KNOW *Polite phrases*

Hier findest du einige nützliche Formulierungen, mit denen du höflich nach etwas fragen oder um etwas bitten kannst.
May I have .../take ...?
Where/How can I find ...?
Shall I help you with/take ...?
What shall I do with ...?
Could you give me .../tell me ..., please?
Is it OK if I invite .../call ...?

2 Stacy is in Oxford now. She is staying with an English host-family.
Write down Stacy's questions for these situations.

1. Stacy wants to phone her parents in America.
2. The tour guide says something to Stacy, but she doesn't understand him because of his English accent.
3. She wants to go to Oxford Museum but doesn't know the way. She asks a lady on the street.
4. The host family's dog is barking because it wants to go for a walk.
5. Stacy's clothes are dirty.
6. Stacy is hungry, but she has to wait for two more hours until the evening meal.
7. Stacy meets another American girl who does not know where she has to go, but Stacy already knows the way.
8. Susan, the other American girl, wants to visit Stacy at her family's house in the evening. Stacy wants to ask her host-mother for permission (= um Erlaubnis bitten)
9. Stacy's host-mother is preparing the evening meal and Stacy wants to help her with it.
10. Stacy wants to write a letter to her best friend in America, but she does not have any paper.

3 Use the connecting words and the past perfect to make one sentence out of two.
When Stacy came back home she told the friends in her rock band about her experiences. They decided to write some songs from what Stacy had written down in her diary. Remember to think: Which action comes first? You also might have to change the order of the clauses.

EXAMPLE

Stacy's friends all read her diary. Then they wrote their first song. (after)
→ *Stacy's friends wrote their first song after they had all read her diary.*

1. They composed many more songs. Then they were satisfied. (not ... until)
2. They practised hard for ten weeks. They had their concert last Saturday. (after)
3. The band could afford the rent for the best hall. A lot of people bought tickets. (because)
4. Stacy's holiday friend Susan left her ticket at home. She wasn't allowed into the concert hall. (because)
5. The girls played their last song. The band left the stage. (after)
6. Susan was in Oxford for a week. She decided to join Stacy's rock band. (when)

Poems

Gedichte müssen sich nicht immer reimen. Sie erzählen eine ganze Geschichte mit wenigen Worten. Oft werden Symbole und Bilder benutzt.

1 Look at this picture. Collect some adjectives that come to your mind.

2 Read poems A to D. Track 5

A
I feel like a dark cloud
So black, wet and sad.
Everything is so loud ...
... I don't want to leave my bed.
A voice keeps calling
Growing increasingly loud.
Rain seems to be falling
From my dark, heavy cloud.
What is this storm?
Today's holy[1] Sunday!
Then I leave my room
And notice it's Monday.
The voice is my mum:
"You'll be late for school!"
What a start to the day ...
... I feel like a fool[2]!

B
Why did it have to go?
I ask myself every day.
Many days in a row[3]
have brought no answer.
It is not here.
There's nothing to change it.
But what do I fear?
Next summer it'll come
THE SUN !!!

[1] holy = heilig, [2] fool = Dummkopf, [3] in a row = hintereinander

C

On the street there lay[1]
– fallen or thrown –
come as it may[2]
a big grass-green stone.

“From where did it come?”
I asked my mum.
“I really don’t know ...
... but it hurt my toe!”

We never will know
about that stone.
My mum said “Let’s go!”
so we walked back home.

D

One two three
why always me?
How did she know?
I didn’t let it show.

Again and again ...
Is she my big fan?
My hope was still there,
I gave her a glare[3].

I wanted a rest
when she passed me the test.
But it quickly turned dark
when I saw my mark.

“You will have to do better!”
– and she passed me a letter
for my dad and my mum.
And gone was the sun ...
... FOREVER

[1] lay = von “*lie*” lag, [2] come as it may = komme, was da wolle, [3] glare = wütender Blick

3 **Listen to the poems on the CD. Match the images below with the poems.**

1

2

3
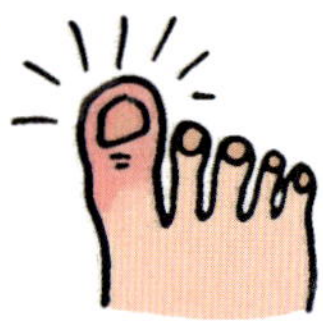

4

5

6

4 **Look at these titles. Which one goes with which poem?**
Can you think of other titles for the four poems?

1	2	3	4
My lucky day?	Alone	Monday morning	Who?

Test

1 The best place to study

Read the following article from a school newspaper. Track 6

What is the best place on earth to study? OXFORD!!!
During my summer holidays I spent six weeks in this wonderful English town.
You probably want to know why I went to Oxford. Well, I read this interesting book, *The Time of My Life*, about a young woman who wanted to study in Oxford in the 19th century. She described the city and its atmosphere so well that I really wanted to go there. I did some research on the internet and found out that the university offers young people from all over the world the opportunity to attend a summer school. This is a project where you can attend lessons and courses like a real student – only for a shorter time. And you do not have to be a real student. I learned that many young English people who have just finished school go to summer school before they enrol for university. Enrolling is when you apply to the university and are accepted as a student there.
Of course it is not easy to find a place to stay. Students can rent a flat or a room, but for six weeks? I wrote an e-mail to the "Student Services" of the university and they really helped me. They gave me the address of a family who wanted to be my host-family for my time in England. I only had to pay a little money for the room and food.
I sent them a letter before I went to Oxford but I was very nervous when I got there.
I didn't know them or the British way of life. Looking back it's really funny that I worried so much, because the family was very nice and friendly. I had lots of fun with them when they showed me Oxford and all the nice places in the area.
If you are thinking of going abroad, do it! I will never forget THE time of MY life!

2 Now tick (✔) the right answer.

1. Stacy thinks Oxford is the best place ...
   - ☐ for holidays.
   - ☐ to study.
   - ☐ to make new friends.
2. She first heard about Oxford through ...
   - ☐ the tourist information.
   - ☐ her mum.
   - ☐ a book.
3. She liked what she got to know about ...
   - ☐ the atmosphere of the city.
   - ☐ the university.
   - ☐ the nightlife.

4. When she needed to find a place to stay in Oxford she was helped by ...
   - ☐ the tourist information.
   - ☐ her mum.
   - ☐ the university.
5. The family Stacy stayed with was ...
   - ☐ unfriendly and impolite.
   - ☐ a little bit strange.
   - ☐ nice and friendly.

You get 1 point for each answer. **Your points:** ____ /5

3 Match the words with the sentences. Be careful with the tenses.

was *should* *had expected* *helped* *should* *read* *had read*
would *enjoyed* *was* *decided* *met* *is* *had enjoyed* *helped*

1. Stacy thinks Oxford ____ the best place on earth to study.
2. She really ____ the book *The Time of My Life*.
3. She ____ to go to Oxford.
4. She wanted to find out if what she ____ was true.
5. The university ____ Stacy to find a home before she came to Oxford.
6. When she left, Stacy's mum told her that she ____ always be polite.
7. Leaving America was more difficult than Stacy ____.
8. But Stacy was not the only one who ____ nervous.
9. The family ____ very nervous too.
10. The family ____ (treffen) her at the airport when she arrived.
11. The children wanted to know what they ____ call her: "Stacy" or "Miss Smith".
12. Stacy had never been called "Miss Smith" before so she said she ____ prefer being called Stacy.
13. Because she remembered the words of her mum, Stacy ____ her host-mother a lot with the housework.
14. Though Stacy ____ (genossen hatte) the book, she found that Oxford was even better in real life.
15. After Stacy had returned to America she ____ *The Time of My Life* again.

You get 1 point for each answer. **Your points:** ____ /15

4 Decide for each sentence which word you have to use in the English sentence for the underlined German word.

would *shall* *should*

1. Tim: Wenn ich Stacy wäre, <u>würde</u> ich einen Regenschirm mit nach England nehmen.
2. Anne: Sie <u>sollte</u> besser auch einen Regenmantel kaufen.
3. Tim: <u>Soll</u> ich dir ein Kapitel aus *The Time of My Life* vorlesen?
4. Tim: Oder <u>würdest</u> du lieber etwas über die Geschichte von London erfahren?
5. Anne: Wenn du so fragst, <u>würde</u> ich lieber etwas über London hören.
6. Anne: Aber du <u>solltest</u> besser deine Hausaufgaben machen, als mir vorzulesen.
7. Anne: <u>Soll</u> ich dir helfen, damit es schneller geht?

You get 1 point for each answer. **Your points:** ____ /7

5 What do you remember? Tick the correct statements about Oxford.

1. The name of the town comes from the times when Saxon farmers crossed the river Thames with their oxen close to the settlement. ☐
2. Oxford is famous for its many different factories. ☐
3. Oxford lies on the river Thames, 60 miles west of London. ☐
4. The first lecture was held in Oxford in 1066. ☐
5. From 1778 on girls were also allowed in Oxford colleges. ☐
6. Nevertheless, girls could not get a degree until 1921. ☐
7. Today many people earn their money with the university, as teachers or in other jobs connected with the students or the college buildings. ☐
8. There are 37 colleges in Oxford altogether. ☐
9. High Street is the main shopping street in Oxford. ☐
10. A punt is a glass of beer. ☐
11. In the summer you can attend summer school in Oxford. ☐
12. As a tourist you are not allowed to go on a boat tour on the river. ☐

You get 1 point for each answer. **Your points:** ____ /12

Your total points out of 39 points: ____

- More than 31? Very good.
- More than 25? Good.
- Less than 19? Have a look at the grammar section and this chapter again. You CAN do better.

3.2 Hören und verstehen

REMEMBER *Listening to texts*

Die wichtigsten Arten von Hörtexten sind Nachrichten (news), Radioberichte (reports/radio broadcasts), Interviews und Hörspiele (radio plays). Richtig zuhören zu können ist aber auch wichtig, wenn man sich unterhält, telefoniert oder einen Anrufbeantworter abhören muss.

Es ist ganz normal, dass du nicht jedes Wort verstehst. Der Trick, um den Text zu verstehen, ist, richtig hinzuhören, sich Notizen zu machen und ihn noch einmal zu hören.

So kannst du aus einem Hörtext Informationen gewinnen:

1. *Before listening*	Lies zuerst den Titel des Hörtextes und – soweit vorhanden – die Hinweise zum Text. Sie geben dir erste Hinweise darauf, worum es in dem Text geht. Manchmal fehlen solche Hinweise jedoch. Jetzt solltest du überlegen, was du schon über das Thema weißt und was du gerne aus dem Text erfahren würdest.
2. *While listening*	Es gibt zwei wichtige Regeln, die man während des Hörens beachten sollte: Mach dir keine Sorgen, wenn du nicht jedes Wort verstehst. Höre einfach auf das, was du verstehen kannst, dann kannst du erraten, worum es geht. Notiere dir auf einem Blatt alles Wichtige in Stichworten. Diese Notizen brauchen nicht geordnet zu sein, denn es muss ja schnell gehen. Wenn der Text fertig ist, ordnest du deine Notizen. Lass ein wenig Platz, denn beim zweiten Hören kannst du dann noch Informationen an der richtigen Stelle ergänzen.
3. *After listening*	Ergänze und sortiere deine Notizen. Schreibe dir an den Rand, welche Stichworte dir bei der Beantwortung welcher Frage helfen.

Horror = L. Dungeon *C. Wren*
places to see:
Trafalgar Square
Buckingham Palace
Underground = Tube *St. Paul's*
red bus *Hyde Park*
1666: fire of London

things to do:	*sights:*	*transport:*
shopping *theatre in Covent Garden* *Hyde Park: relax* *walk along the Thames or go by boat*	*Trafalgar Square* *London Dungeon* *♣ horror museum* *Buckingham Palace* *St. Paul's Cathedral* *built by C. Wren after fire of London in 1666* *Covent Garden* *Hyde Park* *London Eye*	*red buses* *underground* *♣ called "Tube"* *taxi ("cab")*

Modern times – modern families

Track 7

This radio report introduces you to different kinds of modern families. Two teenagers talk about their families and how they have changed.

1 Add information you can get from the title and the introduction above.
Complete the sentences with what you know about the topic. Write in your exercise book.

Title: The text is about ...
The introduction tells me that I will hear a ...
Teenagers will be talking about ....
I know about modern families, that there are ...
The text might tell me more about ...

GOOD TO KNOW *Useful vocabulary*

Hier findest du eine Liste von Wörtern zum Wortfeld „Familie“:

Geschwister	brothers and sisters
Stiefvater/Stiefmutter	stepfather/stepmother
Stiefbruder/-schwester	stepbrother/stepsister
alleinerziehende(r) Mutter/Vater	single mother/father or: single parent
heiraten	to get married/to marry
ihr leiblicher Sohn	her own/natural son
geschiedene Eltern	divorced parents
Scheidung	divorce
Halbbruder	half-brother
Adoptivtochter	adopted daughter
Pflegekind	foster child
Patchworkfamilie	patchwork family
sich verlieben	to fall in love
sich aneinander gewöhnen	to get used to each other
Freunde werden	to become friends
aufwachsen	to grow up

2 Now listen to the text for the first time. Listen to the text for "gist".

Take a piece of paper and take notes. If it is easier for you, listen first and write your notes after the text has ended.

3 Now listen to the text for detail.

Read the questions below. Then listen to the text again. This time concentrate on details and complete your notes. Write down all the information you need to answer the questions.

1. What are the names of the two teenagers?
2. How many people are there in reporter Neil's family? Who are they?
3. Who has got three parents? Who has got four parents?
4. Who is Paul?
5. Neil says he only had one classmate whose parents ...
   - ☐ were still together.
   - ☐ had more than three children.
   - ☐ were divorced.
6. Because times have changed Neil thinks that ...
   - ☐ it is very unusual to have just one parent.
   - ☐ it is not unusual to have just one parent.
   - ☐ lots of parents are unusual.
7. Peter informs us that when his dad went away he thought that ...
   - ☐ it had happened because Peter had done something wrong.
   - ☐ it had happened because his father had done something wrong.
   - ☐ it had happened because his mother had done something wrong.
8. Mary says the good thing about divorced parents is that ...
   - ☐ you have two families.
   - ☐ there is always one of your parents who is nice to you.
   - ☐ they take you to the zoo and buy you ice-cream and toys.
9. Mary tells Neil that she has liked Sally, her dad's new wife, ...
   - ☐ ever since her mother found a new boyfriend.
   - ☐ right from the beginning, because there was no reason for her not to like her.
   - ☐ never, because she caused so much trouble.
10. Mary explains that, with her five brothers and sisters, she will soon have in her family ...
    - ☐ two stepbrothers, two half-sisters and one foster child.
    - ☐ two stepsisters, two half-brothers and one foster child.
    - ☐ one real brother, one stepbrother, two half-sisters and one foster child.

REMEMBER *Reported speech with backshift*

Wenn du – wie im Beispiel unseres Radiointerviews – etwas weitergeben willst, was eine andere Person vor einiger Zeit gesagt hat, verwendest du die **indirekte Rede mit Zeitverschiebung.** Steht das einleitende Verb in der Vergangenheit, kommt es zu einer Zeitverschiebung im folgenden Satz (*backshift*).

Beispiel: Neil: "I'm happy that you **are** here, Mary and Peter."
→ Neil said he was happy that Mary and Peter **were** there.

Regel: Wenn berichtet wird, was jemand zu einem bestimmten Zeitpunkt in der Vergangenheit sagte, schrieb oder dachte, wird die indirekte Rede durch ein Verb des Berichtens im *simple past* (said, wrote, reported, told, ...) eingeleitet.
Die Verbform wird gegenüber der direkten Rede um eine Zeitstufe in die Vergangenheit zurückversetzt. Aus *present* wird *past*, aus *past* wird *past perfect* usw. Personalpronomen, Zeitangaben oder andere Wörter müssen angepasst werden:

yesterday → the day before   for me → for him/her   here → there

Hier siehst du einige Beispiele für die Zeitverschiebung *(backshift):*

am/is/are	→	was/were	present	→	past
is playing	→	was playing	present progressive	→	past progressive
phoned	→	had phoned	past	→	past perfect
have seen	→	had seen	present perfect	→	past perfect
will go	→	would go	*will*-future	→	*would* + infinitive
are going to	→	was/were going to	*going to*-future	→	*was/were* going to + inf.
can	→	could			
may	→	might			

Verbformen, die unverändert bleiben, weil sie nicht weiter in die Vergangenheit zurückversetzt werden können, sind Verben im past perfect sowie could (könnte), would, should und might.

Achtung: Nach said steht kein **Komma,** auch nicht vor that!
That wird oft weggelassen, vor allem nach say und tell.

1 Mary comes home from an interview and tells her parents what Neil was talking about before the interview started.

Fill in the right forms of the verbs in Mary's sentences. The first sentence always shows what Neil said. Remember the backshift! Sometimes you also have to change the personal pronouns or other words.

EXAMPLE

Neil: "I always keep up with the latest style."
→ Mary: "Neil said he *always kept up* with the latest style."

1. Neil: "I'm going to go shopping tomorrow."
   → Mary: "Neil added he ______ shopping the next day."
2. Neil: "My parents gave me all their love."
   → Mary: "Neil told us his parents ______ ______ all their love."
3. Neil: "If I had known that you wanted a poster of *The wonderful 7* I could have organized one for you."
   → Mary: "Neil told me that if he ______ that I wanted a poster of *The wonderful 7* he ______ one for ______."
4. Neil: "I met them yesterday!"
   → Mary: "Neil told me that he ______ them ______."
5. Neil: "I promise I will send you a poster."
   → Mary: "Neil promised he ______ ______ a poster."
6. Neil: "What is your address?"
   → Mary: "Neil asked me what my address ______."
7. Neil: "I've been to this place before!"
   → Mary: "Neil said that he ______ to ______ place before."

GOOD TO KNOW *Expressions of time in reported speech*

Hier ist eine Übersicht über die veränderten Formen von Zeitangaben in der indirekten Rede:

direkte Rede		indirekte Rede
today	→	that day
tomorrow	→	the next/following day
yesterday	→	the day before
next year	→	the next/following year
tonight	→	that night
this evening	→	that evening
three days ago	→	three days before/earlier
last week	→	the week before

2 Dinner at Neil's house

After a long day at the radio station Neil Naff enjoys having dinner with his family. His wife, Mrs Naff, and his children Sarah and Marc usually tell him about their day. Put the introductory verbs into the past tense to make sentences in reported speech. Remember to change time phrases and personal pronouns as well.

EXAMPLE

Mrs Naff: "Our new neighbours are terrible". (say)
→ *Mrs Naff said their new neighbours were terrible.*

1. Mrs Naff: "Children, we are going to watch a good movie tonight." (tell)
2. Neil: "I would like to play cards tomorrow!" (say)
3. Sarah: "We should play cards next week. I want to go to a party tomorrow." (reply)
4. Marc: "You were at two parties last week!" (shout)
5. Mrs Naff: "Marc, you'll be going to parties, too, as soon as you are old enough." (tell)
6. Marc: "I've been to parties before!" (protest)
7. Sarah: "That's true, but you won't be invited again! You broke all the CDs." (answer)
8. Neil: "That's not fair, Sarah. That happened a year ago." (tell)

3 Oh, but didn't you say …?

Mrs Naff is talking to her friend Mrs Cooper.
Complete the answers with the words in brackets. Be careful with the tenses.

1. "We're going to stay at home over Christmas". – "Oh, but you told me you ______ (fly to France for a week)."
2. "The new restaurant is very expensive." – "Is it? I thought you said it ______ (be cheap)."
3. "Sarah likes Paul." – "But she told me ______ (not like Paul very much)."
4. "My husband bought me a new dress." – "Really? You said ______ (buy yourself)."
5. "Perhaps we'll buy a new car." – "Oh, Neil told me you ______ (not buy a new car)."
6. "I painted our kitchen two days ago." – "Well, yesterday you said you ______ (not finish yet)."

REMEMBER *"Say" or "tell"?*

Auf tell folgt immer ein Personenobjekt.
Beispiel: Peter told Marc / me / her / ...

Say steht meist ohne Personenobjekt. Wenn doch ein Personenobjekt folgt, steht es mit to.
Beispiel: Peter said to Marc / me / her / ...

4 Complete the sentences with *say* or *tell* in the correct form.

EXAMPLE

Ann ______ goodbye to me and left. → *Anne said goodbye ...*

1. ______ us about your holiday. Did you have a nice time?
2. Don't just stand there! ______ something!
3. I wonder where Sue is. She ______ she would be here at 8 o'clock.
4. Jack ______ me that he was fed up with his job.
5. The doctor ______ that I should rest for at least a week.
6. Don't ______ anybody what I ______. It's a secret just between us.
7. Did she ______ you what happened? – No, she didn't ______ anything.
8. George couldn't help me. He ______ me to ask Kate.
9. George couldn't help me. He ______ I should ask Kate.

REMEMBER **Fragen in der indirekten Rede**

Steht in der direkten Rede ein Fragewort (what, when, who, why, how, where, ...), behält man es in der indirekten Rede bei. Diese indirekte Rede wird meistens mit dem einleitenden Wort ask begonnen.

Beispiel: Lisa: "**What's** the time, Thomas?" → Lisa asked Thomas what the time was.
Lisa's mother: "**Where were** you, Lisa?" → Lisa's mother asked her **where** she **had been.**

Steht in der direkten Rede kein Fragewort, dann wird der Nebensatz in der indirekten Rede mit if oder whether (= ob) eingeleitet, um zu zeigen, dass es sich um eine Frage handelt.

Beispiel: Thomas: **"Do** you really **want** to go home already?"
→ Thomas asked **whether** Lisa really **wanted** to go home.

Die Wortstellung in indirekten Fragesätzen ist die gleiche wie in Aussagesätzen (Subjekt - Verb - Objekt).

5 After the accident

Neil Naff is making a report on car accidents. He wants to know from an eyewitness (= Augenzeuge) what kind of questions the police asked him after he had seen the accident. Write the questions in reported speech.

Start with: The police asked ...

EXAMPLE

What has happened? → *The police asked what had happened.*

1. Who saw the accident?
2. Have you given first aid (= erste Hilfe)?
3. How many people are hurt?
4. Did you see anything?
5. Where were you when the accident happened?

Neil Naff's answering machine — Track 8

Neil Naff always gets lots of phone calls in his radio studio. Some people want to be on his show, others give him information about important topics for his show. But sometimes Neil is on tour making his reports.
Of course he has got an answering machine (=Anrufbeantworter) to record all the important calls for him. Neil's secretary always listens to the messages and writes them down for him. But somehow it is not her day today. She has made lots of mistakes.

1 Listen to the messages on Neil's answering machine.

Then correct the secretary's mistakes. There are 17 mistakes. Can you find all of them?
Tip: Read the notes before you listen to the answering machine. Then take a pencil and mark the mistakes while you are listening.

Dear Neil,

Here are your messages from the answering machine. You had five calls in total.

1) Susan Saunders, 42 years old, wanted to talk to you about her family. She had listened to the report about modern families. She's from Edinburgh and her house number is 082-774598.

2) Your father called. He wants to talk to you about his 60th birthday. He said it was in four weeks and asked lots of questions about a present, a cake and which suit you were going to wear. Call him back.

3) Bruce has some information for you about a youth centre in Rosemary Road which is in danger of being closed. He said the officials were very upset, because they had no other place to spend their money. Bruce hoped that you could report about it and organize a charity event to raise the money they needed for the centre. The kids from the youth club even offered to clean your studio if you helped them.

4) Mary thanked you for sending her the postcard of The Wonderful 7. She said it was under her bed now. She was very happy that the signatures of all seventeen boys were on it. She said she was a celebrity at school now and some teachers wanted her signature.

2 **Listen to the text again and check whether you have found all the mistakes.**

The race

Track 9

REMEMBER *Backshift – yes or no?*

Die Veränderung der Zeitform ist nicht immer zwingend, aber sie ist nie falsch. Steht jedoch das einleitende Verb im *present tense* (z. B. wenn man über Texte spricht), wird die Zeitform der direkten Rede nicht verändert.

Beispiel: Text: There **are** still cowboys in Dodge City.
→ The text says there **are** still cowboys in Dodge City.

1 **Listen to Neil Naff's commentary (= Live-Reportage) on a vintage car race (= Oldtimer-Autorennen).**
You can listen to the text twice.

2 Right or wrong? Correct the false statements.
Write in your exercise book.

1. It's a wonderful day for the Formula 1 race.
2. The drivers have to be careful because the track is wet and slippery (= rutschig).
3. Kazayoki Yushikato is said to be the most unlucky driver in the race.
4. Lewis Flander's car is grass-green, red and blue.
5. Spencer Speedster is France's big hope.
6. At one point of the race, four cars are level with each other.
7. Renato Pekova is the unlucky driver who crashes with Gilles Grousset.
8. One of the drivers cannot climb out of his car on his own.

3 Fill in the chart.

name	country	colour(s) of car	starting position
Lewis Flanders			
Gilles Grousset			
Letti Hattameki			
Renato Pekova			
Schneider			
Spencer Speedster			
Kazayoki Yushikato			

4 Listen to the text again and check your answers.

5 Finish the sentences in reported speech.

1. Neil said that due to the rain the track was wet and the drivers ______ (müssten vorsichtig sein).
2. He reported that Kazayoki Yushikato was unable to move his car away from the spot so that he ______ (war allen Autos hinter ihm im Weg).
3. Neil told the listeners that Schneider – with his silver racing car – had been able to get out of the way of the spinning car but then Renato Pekova from the Czech Republic ______ (war in Flanders hineingekracht).
4. After the accident Neil ______ (konnte viele grüne, gelbe und lila Autoteile um Pekovas rosafarbenes Auto herumfliegen sehen).
5. Neil informed the audience that they would have a short commercial break and ______ (sie wären dann in wenigen Minuten wieder zurück).

The world of sport

Track 10

1 Listen to the text on the CD.
You can listen to the text several times.

2 Answer the questions below.
Write in your exercise book if there is not enough space.

1. Which sports are explained?
2. What things do you need to do each sport? Make a list of the things that are mentioned in the text!

Be careful: There are many different words for „Schläger“ in English.

3. To which sport do these words belong?
   base
   pitch
   court
   field
   ramp
4. Try to find out with the help of the text what the following words mean:
   oval
   referee
   penalty
   (to) provide
   (to) score
   umpire

3 Guessing game: Which sport is it?

1. It's a game in three parts, of which one is twenty minutes long. You need good protection to play this game since the "ball" is very hard. It can also be quite cold.
2. In this game the referee has to count in a strange way: 15-30-40-game.
3. In order to score a point in this game you have to carry your ball home. Here's a hint: The Americans do have a similar game, but the one we are looking for was invented at a school in England.
4. This game is played with a ball and a bat. Players are dressed completely in white and the game can go on for a long time.
5. And what is the name of the American "brother" of the English game in No. 4?

Test

1 **Listen to Neil Naff's new live report on the CD.** Track 11

2 **Read what you have to do in the exercises below and listen to the text again.**

3 **Now tick the right answers.**

1. Neil Naff's new live report is on a ...
   - ☐ Sunday morning.
   - ☐ Sunday afternoon.
   - ☐ Saturday afternoon.

2. In Rosemary Street there is a ...
   - ☐ youth club.
   - ☐ garage with car wash.
   - ☐ school.

3. The teenagers are washing cars to ...
   - ☐ get more pocket money.
   - ☐ help people.
   - ☐ to help the centre.

4. The centre is important for the teenagers because ...
   - ☐ they can learn to cook in the centre.
   - ☐ many parents have to work late and the kids don't want to be alone at home.
   - ☐ the people in the centre do the homework for the kids.

5. They had the idea of washing cars when ...
   - ☐ they heard Neil's show on the radio.
   - ☐ they talked about the radio show.
   - ☐ they thought of asking Neil and his listeners for help.

6. Neil tells his readers to have their cars washed and ...
   - ☐ to pay £ 5 for it.
   - ☐ that they do not even have to pay for it.
   - ☐ to give as much money as they can spare.

You get 1 point for each correct answer. **Your points:** ______ /6

4 Alison tells her mum about the plan. Tick the right answer.

	A	B
1. Bruce ... he had met Neil last week.	☐ said that	☐ said, that
2. He told Neil that we ... help.	☐ need	☐ needed
3. Neil came when we ... lunch.	☐ had	☐ were having
4. Neil ... that he wanted to help us.	☐ said us	☐ told us
5. He asked me if I ... about the plan	☐ did know	☐ knew
6. He wanted to know if I ... to him in the show.	☐ will talk	☐ would talk
7. I told him we ... grateful for his help.	☐ were	☐ are
8. In the show he asked me what ... doing.	☐ were we	☐ we were
9. Later he said it ... a good idea.	☐ were	☐ was
10. Neil: "I'm going home now." → Neil said he ... home then.	☐ was going	☐ would going

You get 1 point for each correct answer. **Your points:** ____ /10

5 1. Read the following interview by Neil Naff.

Neil: I am talking to the famous pop band *The Wonderful 7*. Tom, when did you first meet the other boys?

Tom: We've known each other since High School. When we first met, we didn't like each other very much. That changed when we played together in the school band.

Neil: That is an interesting story. Tell me, Gerry, how do you feel when you are on stage?

Gerry: I love being on stage. The feeling is great. There was only one concert where I wanted to go home. That was our first concert. Some boys were throwing tomatoes at us.

Neil: Oh no. Jim, you are going to get married, soon. Is that right?

Jim: Yes, that's true. I'm really looking forward to the wedding.

Neil: Your female fans won't be happy about that. Thank you for the interview and good luck for the future.

2. Here is the report that appeared in the newspaper the next day.
Read the text and fill in the gaps (reported speech!).

Radio LBC reporter Neil Naff ____ to *The Wonderful 7* yesterday. He asked Tom when he ____ the other boys for the first time. Tom replied that they ____ each other since High School, but at first they didn't like each other much. Then he added that this ____ when they started playing together in the school band.

When Neil ______ Gerry how he felt when he was on stage, he replied that it was a great feeling. He told Neil the story of their first concert when some boys ______ tomatoes at them.
Neil Naff then wanted to know from Jim ______ it ______ true that he was going to marry soon. Jim said that he ______ looking forward to the wedding.
Neil thought that a lot of female fans ______ be unhappy about that. Finally he ______: "Thank you for the interview!" and wished them good luck for the future.

You get 1 point for each correct answer. **Your points:** ______ /11

6 Backshift – yes or no? Look for the tense of the reporting verb and finish the sentences in the right tense.
Write in your exercise book.

1. I'd like to be in your radio show. → Alison said that ...
2. Too much work isn't good for you. → Neil's mum says that ...
3. I've never been to this youth centre before. → Neil said that ...
4. I like cars. → Bruce says that ...
5. I like washing cars. → Alison said that ...
6. Many politicians don't help the centre anymore. → The poster says ...

You get 1 point for each correct answer. **Your points:** ______ /6

7 *Say* or *tell*? Fill in. Remember to use the correct tense.

1. Yesterday Neil ______ his boss about the car-washing activity in the youth centre.
2. His boss ______ that he had been very satisfied with Neil's radio report.
3. At the moment Neil ______ his boss about the results.
4. He usually ______ his boss about every successful charity event.
5. Last year the boss even ______ Neil to do more for charity.
6. He ______ that this was very good for the image of the radio channel.
7. Neil always prefers ______ his listeners about good things. Bad news always makes him sad.
8. His motto is: Whatever you ______ someone, try ______ it in a friendly way. Friendliness makes the world smile.

You get 1 point for each correct answer. **Your points:** ______ /8

8 Translate these phrases into English.

You can listen to track 7 again if you need help. Words in brackets [ ] do not have to be translated.

1. Ich war sehr verängstigt, weil ich nicht verstand, was [da] passierte.
2. Und was ist mit dir, Mary?
3. In meiner Familie war es dasselbe.
4. Ich war ein Einzelkind und ich mochte es nie.
5. Sie ist ein Pflegekind und lebt mit uns in Lukes Haus.
6. Das hört sich nach viel (= gutem) Spaß an.
7. Ich mochte sie am Anfang [gar] nicht, weil sie so viel Ärger verursacht hatte.
8. Das Gute an geschiedenen Eltern ist, dass beide extrem nett zu dir sein wollen.
9. Ich wuchs in einer eher normalen Familie auf, würde ich sagen.
10. Möchtest du uns davon erzählen?

You get 2 points for each correct answer. **Your points:** /20

9 Which words go together? Match the German and the English words.

1. Geschwister	A to grow up
2. Scheidung	B stepfather
3. sich aneinander gewöhnen	C stepbrother
4. aufwachsen	D half-brother
5. alleinerziehender Elternteil	E divorce
6. Stiefvater	F brothers and sisters
7. Adoptivkind	G foster child
8. Pflegekind	H single parent
9. Halbbruder	I adopted child
10. Stiefbruder	J to get used to each other

You get 1 point for each correct answer. **Your points:** ______ /10

Your total points out of 71 points: ______

- More than 66? Very good.
- More than 50? Good.
- Less than 36? Have a look at this chapter again. You CAN do better.

4 Texte schreiben

Das musst du am Ende der Klasse 7 können:

- ▷ Zu vertrauten Themen zusammenhängende Texte, Briefe und Tagebucheinträge verfassen
- ▷ Bildvorgaben oder Absichten versprachlichen
- ▷ Durch das Entwickeln von Fragen Informationen ermitteln
- ▷ Texte zusammenfassen, nacherzählen, fortführen, ergänzen oder Alternativen dazu schriftlich darstellen

4.1 Mit Satzbausteinen Texte erstellen

GOOD TO KNOW *Guided writing*

Wenn du anhand von vorgegebenen Textbausteinen Texte erstellen sollst, musst du oftmals Verben, Adjektive oder Nomen ergänzen und auf die richtige Stellung im Satz achten.
Textbausteine sind eine Hilfe bei der Erstellung von Texten. Die Bausteine geben dir erste Informationen darüber, wovon dein Text handeln soll. Verwende alle Bausteine. Sie ergeben oft aber erst dann einen Sinn, wenn du weitere Wörter hinzufügst.
Um einen Text besonders interessant oder spannend zu schreiben, solltest du möglichst viele **Adjektive** verwenden. Beschreibe, was die Personen deiner Geschichte sehen, hören oder riechen können. So kann sich der Leser deiner Geschichte besser in die Handlung hineinversetzen.

1 Compare the sentences below. Which one do you think is better? Why?

1. It was a cold, dark night with an icy wind howling from the mountains, and Lisa felt terribly scared.
2. Because it was night and the wind was blowing Lisa felt scared.

2 Do you remember Sir Francis Drake? Another famous English sailor was Sir Walter Raleigh.

He lived from 1554 to 1618. Of course he made entries in his logbook on all his journeys. Use the notes to write the logbook entry (= Eintrag) of Sir Walter Raleigh's journey. Put the building blocks (= Textbausteine) in the correct order to form complete sentences. Each sentence begins with a capital letter and ends with a full stop.

EXAMPLE

on the sea.	was	It	another windy day

It was another windy day on the sea.

Day forty-five

1.	the coast.	In a few days	will reach	we
2.	Eldorado, the City of Gold.	There	hope to find	I
3.	for more than forty days.	have been	We	on this ship
4.	land	again,	want to see	The men
	the only thing	every day	we can see	is water.
	but			
5.	are	Some men	sea-sick (=seekrank)	
	in this region.	the many storms	because of	
6.	a dead rat	Yesterday	we found	
	nearly all our bacon.	had eaten	and it	
7.	is useless,	What is left	was ill.	the rat
	because			
8.	the rest of the bacon	into the sea.	had to throw	We
9.	nearly all our fresh water.	have also	drunk	We
10.	a good meal	I dream of	fresh bread,	and
	on the ship.	there is	because	not much left
11.	illnesses	in the New World	have	Many people
	in England.	do not have	we	that
12.	a doctor	on this ship.	have brought	we
	for them	So		

4.2 Briefe verfassen

REMEMBER *Informal letters* – Briefe an Familie, Freunde und Bekannte

Wenn du einen Brief schreibst, solltest du dir zuerst überlegen, worüber du schreiben möchtest. Es hilft, wenn du dir Notizen machst. Dies ist dann besonders hilfreich, wenn du in einem Antwortbrief auf Themen eingehen willst, die in dem Brief stehen, den du bekommen hast. So vergisst du später beim Schreiben nichts und kannst deinen Brief nach verschiedenen Themen ordnen. Ein Brief hat immer den gleichen Aufbau. Zuerst kommt die **Anrede**, in der du den Namen des Adressaten nennst, dann dein **Text** und am Schluss nette **Grußworte** und deine **Unterschrift**.

Je nachdem, an wen der Brief versendet wird, müssen Anrede, Grußworte sowie Inhalt des Briefes angepasst werden.

- Wenn du einen Brief beantworten möchtest, solltest du dir zuerst in Stichworten notieren, auf welche Punkte du antworten möchtest.
- Die Anrede ist persönlich, z. B. Dear Sarah. Nach der Anrede steht ein Komma und du schreibst in der nächsten Zeile groß weiter (anders als im Deutschen!).
- In deinem Text darfst du umgangssprachliche Begriffe sowie Kurzformen (I'm) und unkomplizierte, kurze Sätze verwenden.
- Zum Schluss wählst du passende Grußworte (siehe Kasten unten) aus, je nachdem, wie gut du den Adressaten kennst. Vergiss das Komma nach dem Grußwort nicht und unterschreibe mit deinem Vornamen.

Beispiel:

Dear Sarah,
Thank you for your last letter. I hope you are well.
Your holidays must have been great. Mine were good, too. I went on a holiday where I did lots of horse-riding. I slept in a big house with a lot of other children and every day we had riding lessons. It was great fun.
But now school has started again. My teachers are OK. The English teacher is cool, but I don't like my maths teacher very much. What is your favourite subject?

Please write back soon.
Love,
Tina

GOOD TO KNOW **Nützliche Bausteine für einen Brief**

Dear ...,
Thank you for your postcard/letter.
I'm glad to hear from you after all this time.
I hope you are doing well. I'm fine.
I am having a great time in ...
In the photo I'm sending you you can see ...
I have to tell you what happened to me last Friday/week/month ...
You won't believe it but I really ...
Please write back soon./I hope to hear from you soon.
Have a good holiday/time in .../Enjoy your first school week/...
Love, .../Bye, .../Best wishes, .../Lots of love, .../All the best, .../Yours, ...

1 Sarah's first day at the new school

Sarah wants to write a letter to her German friend Tina. Here are her notes. Please write the letter in your exercise book and try to use these notes.

- thank her for letter
- good that she enjoyed holidays
- we're back at school, too
- ask Tina if I told her that I'm at new school – first day yesterday – really nervous
- mum and dad took me by car – first had to go to head teacher – nice, name: Mrs Thompson – showed me how to get to new class
- all kids in class new – we're in secondary school now – like German "Gymnasium" (so far I attended primary school, stayed there for 6 years)
- great: to be old enough – new school – lots of cute older boys
- new classmates: nice
- teachers: seem OK, too – only chemistry teacher (Mr Whitehead) strange – old – smells. Yuck!
- later: went to cafeteria (have lunch), some older girls pushed us around, said we were sitting at their table. Samantha – really ugly & terrible, took bottle of ketchup & squeezed it all over my chips – couldn't eat them anymore, but was lucky – chemistry teacher saw it, shouted at her
- she had to buy new chips for me & he sent her to detention (= you have to stay longer at school after lessons/extra work/think about what you have done wrong). Ha-ha!
- Mr Whitehead not so bad after all?
- Ask Tina to tell – about her first day at school – hope she had better start
- write soon

2 Here is Tina's answer. But the sentences have been jumbled. Try to bring them into the correct order.

Dear Sarah,

1. *for* | *Thank you* | *funny* | *letter* | *your*
2. *must really* | *first day* | *have* | *exciting* | *your* | *been*
3. *because I* | *my* | *interesting* | *school,* | *the Stadtgymnasi-um* | *Mine wasn't* | *still go* | *to my old*
4. *But* | *after* | *to see* | *holidays* | *my friends* | *the long* | *it was nice* | *again*
5. *The first lesson* | *was* | *my favourite* | *maths* | *which is not* | *of the day* | *subject*

6. *because* *first day* *are allowed* *home* *We were lucky* *after the holidays* *to go* *on* *the* *we* *early*

7. *went to* *my friends and I* *some of* *After school* *an ice-cream parlour.*

8. *was* *fun* *It* *great*

9. *as soon as possible* *delicious ice-cream* *The parlour has* *so* *we are planning* *to go there* *again*

10. *together* *have to visit* *during the next holidays,* *then* *You really* *me* *we can go there*

11. *all the news* *and* *with chemistry* *tell me* *please* *Have fun*

Lots of love,
Tina

3 Match the German and English phrases for letters.

1. Enjoy your ...
2. Thank you for your ...
3. Dear ...
4. I hope to hear from you soon.
5. I'm glad to hear from you.
6. Love, ...
7. All the best, ...
8. Yours, ...
9. Bye, ...
10. Best wishes, ...

A Ich hoffe, ich höre bald von dir.
B Alles Gute, ...
C Alles Liebe, ...
D Viele Grüße, ...
E Danke für deine(n) ...
F Ich bin froh, von dir zu hören.
G Tschüss, ...
H Liebe(r) ...
I Genieß deine(n) ...
J Dein(e), ...

REMEMBER *Possessive pronouns instead of nouns*

Du verwendest Possessivpronomen statt des bekannten Nomens, um Wiederholungen zu vermeiden.
Wie die Possessivbegleiter (*possessive determiners*: my, your usw.) geben die Possessivpronomen (*possessive pronouns:* mine, yours usw.) an, wem etwas gehört.
Ist das Nomen aus einem vorhergehenden Satz bekannt, musst du es nicht nochmals wiederholen. Dann kannst du das passende Possessivpronomen verwenden.
Beispiele:
Is this **my** English book? – No, sorry. It's **mine**.
David, here is **your** ticket. – Thanks mum. Have you got **yours**, too?

Do you like **their** Halloween costumes? – Yes, but **theirs** aren't as scary as mine.
statt: → Yes, but their Halloween costumes aren't as scary as my Halloween costume.

Hier findest du Beispiele für verschiedene Possessivpronomen:

		Possessive determiner + noun	*Possessive pronoun*
I	→ mine	This is my sandwich.	→ No, it's mine.
you	→ yours	Can you lend me your pen?	→ Yes, of course. But this is yours anyway.
he	→ his	Let's have a look at his photos.	→ Yes, his are always the best.
she	→ hers	Is that her boyfriend at the door?	→ No, hers is sitting on the sofa.
we	→ ours	Is this our car?	→ No, it's not. Ours is parked over there.
you	→ yours	Is that your child in the sea?	→ No, it's yours. Ours can't swim yet.
they	→ theirs	Do you like their food?	→ Yes, but theirs is not as healthy as ours.

1 Put in the correct possessive pronoun.
Sarah spent her last school holidays in Scotland with her family and her uncle Craig. In one of her letters she tells Tina about it.

1. You told me about your holidays, so let me now tell you about ________.
2. We have a lot of relatives all over the UK and we like to visit them. I don't know where your family's relatives live, ________ live in Scotland.
3. Uncle Craig owns a house in Scotland – it's ________.
4. Mum lived in another house when she was young. Since her parents died, it has been ________. But it's too small for all of us.
5. So we went to stay with Uncle Craig and his dog Pete. We also took our dog Lucy, so that his dog could play with ________.

6. Is ______ a friendly dog, too? ______ is a really good girl.
7. My grandparents also have two dogs but ______ are really dangerous. They bite other dogs if you aren't careful.
8. One day we wanted to go to the next town with Uncle Craig but his car was broken so we had to take ______. It was a problem because our car isn't as big as ______.

2 Translate these sentences from Tina's letter into English. Use as many possessive determiners and pronouns as possible.

Poor Sarah. She receives an answer from Tina, but Tina didn't remember to write her letter in English. Sarah doesn't speak German, so she needs someone to translate the letter for her.

1. Vielen Dank für deinen Brief, hier kommt meiner.
2. Als ich deinen gelesen habe, musste ich lachen.
3. Deine Familie ist genau wie unsere.
4. In unserer gibt es auch viele Hunde.
5. Ich mag fast alle, außer (=except) den Hund von meiner Tante. Der ist wirklich schrecklich. Schlimmer als unserer.
6. Nicht viele Hunde mögen es, mit Katzen zu spielen. Mag deiner Katzen?
7. Unsere Nachbarn haben auch Wellensittiche (= budgies). Ihre sind blau und weiß.

3 Tina also sent some photos with her letter.

She wrote some sentences on the back of the photos, so that Sarah knows what they show.

Change the sentences, using possessive determiners or pronouns instead of nouns.

EXAMPLE

My grandparents' house is green. → *Their house* is green.
That bike is my bike. → That bike is *mine*.

1. The blue room is my brother's room.
2. My room is pink.
3. My parents' bedroom has got a green ceiling.
4. Our living-room is really big.
5. Our neighbours' garden is smaller than our garden.
6. Sarah's favourite place is next to the window.
7. Dad's seat is the big armchair.
8. The rabbits' favourite place is in the garden.
9. Where is your favourite place?
10. And where is your parents' favourite place?

4.3 Bildergeschichten schreiben

GOOD TO KNOW **Tipps zum Schreiben einer Bildergeschichte**

Eine spannende Art des Geschichtenschreibens ist das Schreiben einer Bildergeschichte. Oft sind Bilder vorgegeben, manchmal auch Satzbausteine oder Notizen, die dir den Einstieg erleichtern.
Bilder geben nur den groben Rahmen für eine Geschichte vor. Du kannst dazuerfinden, was du möchtest, solange du die Folge der Bilderinhalte beachtest. Adjektive machen deine Geschichte lebendiger. Durch Einblicke in die Gedanken deiner Personen wirkt deine Geschichte spannender.

- Zunächst solltest du dir die **Bilder** genau **ansehen** und dir eine passende Geschichte dazu überlegen. Dann kannst du dir auf einem Blatt erste **Notizen** machen, damit du beim Schreiben nichts vergisst.
- Schreibe nicht zu viel zu jedem einzelnen Bild. Deine Geschichte sollte für deine Leser einfach nachzuvollziehen sein.
- Um die Geschichte besonders abwechslungsreich zu gestalten, sollest du auch **wörtliche Rede** verwenden. Auf diese Weise kannst du deine Leser an den Gedanken deiner Figuren teilhaben lassen.
- Spannend werden Bildergeschichten, wenn sie ein überraschendes Ende haben.

1 **Finish writing the picture story about Peter and the ghost.**
One scary Saturday ...

EXAMPLE

1. It all happened on a Saturday evening. Peter was alone at home because his parents were visiting his grandparents. "Great!", Peter thought. "I can watch the horror film. Mum would never let me watch it if she was here." It was an exciting evening. Peter was sitting on the sofa and the film was very scary. It was about a horrifying white ghost which hid behind sofas and under beds in people's houses and scared them to death.
2. The longer Peter watched, the more frightened he became. Suddenly he had a strange feeling, as if he wasn't alone anymore. "Hello? Hell-oooo?" he asked with a thin voice. "Is anybody there?" From behind him came a strange sound and his back felt very cold. It was as if an icy wind was blowing down his neck. It clearly came from behind the sofa, but at first Peter didn't dare look to see what it was.
3. ...

2 Look at the pictures below.
Here are more pictures. This time it is a mystery story. That is a story in which something strange happens and a problem has to be solved. There is no real ending to the story.

3 Write a mystery story. Use the words given below.
You do not have to use the words in the given order. You can add any other words you like. Then write a good ending to the story.

EXAMPLE

One day, when Tina came home from school, she noticed a letter sticking out of the letter box. She was expecting a letter from her friend. ...

1. *letter* *letter box* *excited*
2. *Tina* *cannot wait* *open* *read* *envelope* *pen-friend* *strange story* *terrible incident* (= Vorfall)
3. *Tina* *read* *letter* *her room* *quiet* *apart from* (= abgesehen von) *bird* *sing* *mother* *call* *dinner* *re* *leave* *desk*
4. *When* *come back* *room* *realize* (= feststellen) *letter* *was gone* *strange* *who* *steal?*

REMEMBER *Irregular verbs* – unregelmäßige Verben

Wenn du Geschichten über bereits vergangene Ereignisse schreibst, benutzt du meist das *simple past*.
Regelmäßige Verben haben in allen Vergangenheitsformen die Endung -ed.
Beispiel: He played football yesterday.

Die **unregelmäßigen Verben** musst du gut kennen, denn deren Vergangenheitsform kann man nicht ableiten. Man muss sie auswendig lernen.
Eine Liste der unregelmäßigen Verben findest du in deinem Schulbuch (meistens auf den letzten Seiten).

Bei manchen unregelmäßigen Verben sind alle drei Formen (*infinitive*, *simple past* und *past participle*) gleich.
Beispiel: das Verb hit (= schlagen):

Don't **hit** me. → *infinitive*
Somebody **hit** me as I came into the room. → *simple past*
I'**ve** never **hit** anybody in my whole life. → *present perfect* (*past participle*)
Tommy **was hit** on the head by a stone. → *passive voice* (*past participle*)

Hier ist eine Tabelle mit einigen Verben, bei denen alle drei Formen gleich sind:

(to) cost	cost, cost	kosten
(to) hit	hit, hit	schlagen, treffen
(to) hurt	hurt, hurt	verletzen, weh tun
(to) let	let, let	lassen
(to) put	put, put	setzen, stellen, legen
(to) read	read, read **Achtung:** Hier werden die 2. und die 3. Form „red" ausgesprochen.	lesen

Bei den meisten unregelmäßigen Verben sind die zweite (*simple past*) und die dritte Form (*past participle*) gleich, unterscheiden sich aber von der Grundform (*infinitive*).

Beispiel: das Verb tell (= erzählen):

Can you **tell** me what to do? → *infinitive*

She **told** me to come again the next day. → *simple past*

Have you **told** anyone about your new bike? → *present perfect* (*past participle*)

I **was told** to come back the next day. → *passive voice* (*past participle*)

Hier ist eine Tabelle mit einigen Verben, bei denen die 2. und 3. Form gleich sind:

(to) bleed	bled, bled	bluten
(to) bring	brought, brought	bringen
(to) build	built, built	bauen
(to) buy	bought, bought	kaufen

Hier ist eine Tabelle mit einigen Verben, bei denen die 1. und 3. Form gleich sind:

(to) become	became, become **Achtung:** Nicht zu verwechseln mit to get!	werden
(to) come	came, come	kommen
(to) run	ran, run	rennen, laufen

Einige unregelmäßige Verben haben drei verschiedene Formen.

Beispiel: das Verb wake (up) (= (auf-)wecken, (auf-)wachen)

I'll **wake** you up. → *infinitive*

I **woke** up in the middle of the night. → *simple past*

Listen, the baby **has woken** up! → *present perfect* (*past participle*)

I **was woken** up by a loud noise. → *passive voice* (*past participle*)

Hier ist eine Liste mit unregelmäßigen Verben, bei denen alle drei Formen verschieden sind:

(to) fly	flew, flown	fliegen
(to) give	gave, given	geben
(to) know	knew, known	wissen, kennen
(to) ride	rode, ridden	fahren, reiten
(to) show	showed, shown	zeigen

Einige wenige Verben können sowohl unregelmäßig als auch regelmäßig sein.
Beispiel: das Verb dream (= träumen)
Do you usually **dream** at night? → *infinitive*
I **dreamt/dreamed** about you last night. → *simple past*
Have you ever **dreamt/dreamed** that before? → *present perfect* (*past participle*)
The dream was **dreamt/dreamed earlier**. → *passive voice* (*past participle*)
Beachte: Im britischen Englisch ist bei solchen Verben die unregelmäßige Form (dreamt, sprich: [dremt]) üblicher, im amerikanischen Englisch wird eher die regelmäßige Form (dreamed) benutzt.

Hier ist eine Liste von Verben, die sowohl regelmäßig als auch unregelmäßig sein können:

(to) burn	burnt/burned, burnt/burned	(ver)brennen
(to) dream	dreamt/dreamed, dreamt/dreamed	träumen (dreamt, sprich: [dremt])
(to) lean	leant/leaned, leant/leaned	(sich) lehnen, (vor)beugen (leant, sprich: [lent])
(to) learn	learnt/learned, learnt/learned	lernen (learnt, sprich: [lernt])
(to) spell	spelt/spelled, spelt/spelled	buchstabieren, richtig schreiben

1 **Fill in the gaps with the missing irregular verb forms.**

	Infinitive	Simple Past	Past Participle	German
1.	sing			
2.		read		
3.			caught	
4.				wachsen
5.		hit		
6.	overtake			
7.				erzählen
8.			lost	

9.	hurt			
10.		drank		
11.	write			
12.				zeigen
13.			sent	
14.			built	
15.		felt		
16.	sleep			
17.				lassen
18.	buy			
19.		left		
20.				unterrichten
21.				tun, machen
22.		sat		
23.			had	
24.				behalten, aufbewahren
25.	bring			
26.				schütteln, zittern
27.			seen	
28.		wore		
29.	steal			
30.			flown	
31.		chose		
32.	eat			
33.			forgotten	
34.				geben
35.			gone	
36.	hide			
37.		left		
38.				verlieren
39.		paid		
40.				laufen
41.	shoot			
42.		spent		
43.			stood	
44.			swum	
45.				werfen

2 Fill in the correct form of the verbs in brackets.

Louise went on a school trip with her class. The boys and girls spent five days in a youth hostel. After they returned home, she told her mother about it.

1. We ______ (not know) that the journey on the bus would be so long, but we ______ (have) a good time. I ______ (talk) to Lisa and Mary nearly all the time. We ______ (eat) lots of sweets, until the bus driver ______ (shout) at us. He ______ (say) it was forbidden to eat on the bus. We ______ (not drink) anything either. It was also forbidden.
2. When we ______ (arrive) at the youth hostel, Mrs Robinson ______ (find) £10 in the street. She ______ (take) it to the police station, but they ______ (not want) it. They ______ (say) they wouldn't find the person who had ______ (lose) it anyway, and ______ (give) it back to her. So Mrs Robinson ______ (send) us to the ice-cream parlour and ______ (pay) for our ice-cream. That was great and it really ______ (cost) a lot of money.
3. We ______ (not do) much the next day. The weather ______ (not be) very good, so we ______ (stay) in our rooms, ______ (read), ______ (sing) some songs, ______ (write) a few postcards and just ______ (hang) around. But then Mrs Robinson ______ (get) angry with us because our rooms ______ (look) so messy (= unordentlich) and she ______ (make) us tidy up our things.
4. During the night some of the boys ______ (come) around to our room to visit us. They even ______ (bring) some playing cards which they had ______ (buy) in the afternoon. But then Mr Davenport ______ (catch) us. He had ______ (hear) us laughing, so he ______ (leave) his bed and ______ (run) into our room. He ______ (hurt) his leg on one of the bedposts (= Bettpfosten) and ______ (fall) right into Paula's arms. It was very funny at first, but in the end poor Mr Davenport ______ (spend) the rest of the night in hospital and Mrs Robinson ______ (sleep) in our room with us.
5. When we ______ (get) up next morning she ______ (tell) us that she ______ (think) Mr Davenport would have to stay in hospital for two more days. She ______ (sit) down on a chair and ______ (explain) to us that we ______ (have) to return home. We ______ (understand), ______ (pack) our bags and ______ (leave) the youth hostel. We all ______ (feel) very sad when we ______ (get) on the bus.

3 Write another mysterious story and find a good ending.

REMEMBER *Useful vocabulary: connectives*

Connectives sind Wörter oder Wortgruppen, die Sätze verbinden. Sie können auch am Satzanfang stehen.
Hier ist eine Liste von Ausdrücken, die du verwenden kannst, um Sätze zu verbinden oder zu beginnen:

all in all	alles in allem
although	obwohl
and	und
anyway	sowieso, nun denn (am Satzanfang)
apart from	abgesehen von
as a result	folglich, infolgedessen
as well ... as	sowohl ... als auch, nicht nur ... sondern auch
at the same time	zur selben/gleichen Zeit
because	weil
besides	außerdem, noch dazu
but	aber
finally	schließlich, zuletzt, zum Schluss
for that reason	aus diesem Grund
from now on	von jetzt an
furthermore	darüber hinaus
however	wie auch immer, wie dem auch sei, jedoch
in addition	zusätzlich, es kommt hinzu
in case	für den Fall, dass ...
in order to	um zu
in spite of	trotz
in the first place	zuerst, an erster Stelle
indeed	tatsächlich, in der Tat, wirklich
little by little	nach und nach
meanwhile	in der Zwischenzeit, unterdessen, mittlerweile
moreover	darüber hinaus
nevertheless	nichtsdestoweniger, trotzdem
not only ... but also	nicht nur ... sondern auch
on second thoughts	wenn ich es mir recht überlege, nach reiflicher Überlegung
on the other hand	andererseits, auf der anderen Seite
on top of that	obendrein, darüber hinaus
so	sodass

4.4 Zeitungsartikel schreiben

REMEMBER **Merkmale eines Zeitungsartikels**

Zeitungsartikel **informieren** umfassend über ein Thema oder eine Geschichte. Sie sind in **sachlicher,** klarer Sprache geschrieben (keine Umgangssprache!).

Die sechs wichtigsten Fragen, die ein Zeitungsbericht (= report) beantworten sollte, sind:

- Who? → Wer?
- What? → Was?
- Where? → Wo?
- When? → Wann?
- Why? → Warum?
- How? → Wie?

Zeitungsartikel haben fast immer den gleichen Aufbau:

1. Überschrift (= *headline*) → informiert über das Thema des Artikels
2. Einleitung (= *introduction*) → gibt die wichtigsten Informationen an (who, what, where, when?)
3. Mittelteil (= *main part*) → enthält weitere interessante Einzelheiten zum Thema
4. Schluss (= *end*) → Hier kann man hilfreiche Ratschläge oder Informationen zum Thema geben (**Achtung:** Keine eigene Meinung!).

Sprachliche Besonderheiten:

- Die Überschrift sollte kurz sein, das Interesse der Leser wecken und enthält in der Regel keine Artikel. Meist wird die Überschrift im *simple present* formuliert.
  Beispiel: Joker breaks into Madame Tussaud's (= Witzbold bricht bei Madame Tussaud's ein)
- Berichtet der Artikel über ein Ereignis aus der Vergangenheit, steht der Text im *simple past*. Geht es um allgemeine Informationen, behält man im Text wie in der Überschrift das *simple present* bei.
- Oft wird in Zeitungsartikeln das Passiv verwendet, z. B. wenn unbekannt ist, wer der Täter war.
  Beispiel: A lot of money was stolen.

EXAMPLE A report

Joker[1] breaks into Madame Tussaud's

A curious incident happened at Madame Tussaud's in London last Saturday. Unknown people broke into the famous museum and stole the wax-figure of Prince Charles. The police searched for it for more than five hours. They finally found it … in the garden of Buckingham Palace. It seems that someone had thought it funny to place the wax figure there. It had been given new clothes as well: instead of Prince Charles's suit – which had once been donated by the Prince himself – the figure wore a carnival dress.

Prince Charles "walking" around Buckingham Palace gardens dressed up[2] as a horse – a joke aimed at his wife Camilla? No matter whether YOU can laugh about this "joke" – it is a crime and should not be copied!

The police in London think that it must have been two or three people who committed the crime[3]. "These wax figures are heavy – you couldn't possibly carry one of them alone!", said Mike Maxwell, Police Officer.

If the culprits[4] are caught they will be punished with a few years in prison. If you know anything about the deed, please contact your local police station, or call us on 892-5629.

[1] joker = Witzbold, [2] (to) dress up as = verkleiden als, [3] (to) commit a crime = ein Verbrechen begehen, [4] culprits = Täter

Buckingham Palace, London

Prince Charles and his wife Camilla, at Madame Tussaud's

GOOD TO KNOW **Tipps zum Schreiben eines Zeitungsartikels**

Willst du einen Zeitungsartikel schreiben, kannst du folgendermaßen vorgehen:

1. **Brainstorming** → Schreibe in Stichworten auf, was dir zu dem Thema einfällt.
2. Gruppiere die Stichwörter dann sinnvoll nach übergeordneten Themen.
   Tipp: Wenn du jedes Stichwort auf einen kleinen Zettel schreibst, kannst du sie später besser sortieren. Daraus kannst du eine **Gliederung** erstellen.
3. Nun schreibst du mithilfe deiner Gliederung deinen Artikel. Achte darauf, den Text in sinnvolle **Absätze** zu unterteilen.
4. Der letzte Schritt ist die sprachliche Überarbeitung deines Textes. Achte besonders auf die **richtigen Zeiten** und die Verwendung des **Passivs.** Du kannst auch ein Wörterbuch zu Hilfe nehmen, z. B. um Wörter zu verwenden, die du nur im Deutschen kennst, oder um treffendere Wörter für umgangssprachliche Begriffe zu finden. Wenn du Zeit hast, solltest du einen Tag warten, bevor du deinen Artikel sprachlich verbesserst, da dir dann möglicherweise mehr auffällt.
5. Folgende Fragen helfen bei der **Selbstkontrolle** aller eigenen Texte:
   - Bleibe ich im gesamten Text bei meiner Erzählzeit (z. B. *simple present*)?
   - Habe ich kurze, verständliche Sätze geschrieben?
   - Habe ich an die richtige Schreibweise und an die unregelmäßigen Verben gedacht?

1 Violence at a British school

Read the following interview and listen to it on the CD. **Track 12**

Interviewer: I am now talking to the headmaster of Rosemary School in Bristol. Mr Adams, can you tell me why you had to call the police last Friday?

Headmaster: Yes, of course. It's unbelievable. Some of my teachers had told me about a new habit of our pupils. You know that nowadays young people don't go anywhere without their mobile phones. Well, we saw them standing around in the break, looking at the mobile of one of the boys. It was the way they were looking at it that was strange.
So I went outside to see what was on it.

Interviewer: What did you find when you looked at the mobile?

Headmaster: I couldn't believe my eyes. They had a film scene where some boys beat up a younger boy. It was only later that I realized that this fight had taken place at my school, here in Bristol.

Interviewer: How old were the boys?

Headmaster: Well, the poor one that was beaten up was only ten years old. The boys who gave him a hard time were older, two of them were already 15 years old, three of them between 13 and 14. And all of them were pupils at this

	school. Nice boys, it seemed. Who could have imagined what terrible things they did after school?
Interviewer:	Did you find out why they hit the boy?
Headmaster:	That's the most terrible thing I ever heard a young person say. The boys explained that it hadn't been a matter of having arguments. They thought it was just a joke, to film how they hurt him. They had chosen this pupil because he was rather weak and couldn't defend himself. They just wanted to shoot a good film to show their friends. Can you believe that?
Interviewer:	Indeed, violent scenes on mobile phones are a problem in Great Britain. It is cool to have such a film on your mobile, the more violent the better. Young people send the films from mobile to mobile. It's like a competition, everyone wants to have the most violent film. And the losers are the victims. Mr Adams, how do you want to improve the situation at your school?
Headmaster:	The boys are now facing punishment. Of course, they are too young to go to court, but the police have agreed with the parents that the boys will have to do some hours of community service in their free time.
Interviewer:	What exactly does that mean?
Headmaster:	They will have to help in an animal refuge, that's a home for pets without owners. We hope that the work with these poor animals will teach them that violence is not cool.
Interviewer:	And what about all the other young people at your school?
Headmaster:	As a first step, mobile phones are not allowed at my school anymore. The kids have to leave them at home. I think, the real problem is that the children see a lot of violence on TV. They are so used to it and don't know how terrible it is and how much it hurts. So we also started a programme called "Stop the aggression". This way we want to teach them that doing sports or playing games in the real world is much better than watching TV or playing computer games in your free time. We also had an information evening for the parents, where we advised them to check their children's mobile phones from time to time. "Know what your child does", that's the slogan!
Interviewer:	And it's the best thing parents can do! Thank you, Mr Adams.

2 Write a report about violence at a British school.
Use the information given in the interview with the headmaster of the school. Remember to use connectives to make your text sound good. You may also include quotations (= Zitate) but you should mainly use your own words.

4.5 Die eigene Meinung äußern

GOOD TO KNOW **So gehst du vor**

Wenn du mit jemandem über einen Film sprichst, den du gesehen hast, teilst du ihm meist auch deine eigene Meinung darüber mit. Auch über Bücher, Spiele oder bestimmte Themen kann man anderen seine Meinung mitteilen.

Sicherlich hast du schon einmal von einem Freund oder einer Freundin ein Buch, einen Film oder ein Spiel empfohlen bekommen. Wenn man eine Empfehlung oder seine eigene Meinung über etwas äußert, verwendet man ganz bestimmte Formulierungen.

Da sich Bücher, Filme usw. nie verändern, auch wenn man sie mehrmals liest oder sieht, benutzt man immer das ***simple present***, wenn man darüber spricht oder schreibt.

Empfehlungen oder Meinungsäußerungen haben oft den gleichen Aufbau:

1. Zuerst äußert man seine Empfehlung oder Meinung.
   Beispiele: You really should read that book! It's brilliant.
   If I were you, I wouldn't watch that film. You'll just fall asleep!
2. Dann begründet man, warum man so denkt. Je genauer die Begründung ist, desto leichter kann sich der andere ein Bild davon machen, ob er auch so denkt. Schließlich sind Filme, Bücher usw. auch immer Geschmackssache.
3. Eine kleine Zusammenfassung des Inhaltes kann dabei helfen, sich zu entscheiden, ob der Film oder das Buch einem gefallen könnte.
4. Zum Schluss kann man noch einmal auf die Empfehlung vom Anfang zurückkommen.

EXAMPLE Eine Buchempfehlung

Have you read *Harry Potter* by Joanne K. Rowling? If you haven't, you really should. It's the best story I've ever read. It's very long, because it consists of seven books, but each book is really exciting and you can read one after the other. The language is not too difficult, so you can read the books quickly.
They are about a young boy whose parents died when he was a baby. He lives with his aunt and uncle but is unhappy because they treat him badly. Then he finds out that he is a wizard.
He attends a boarding school for young wizards and witches, Hogwarts, to learn how to do magic. He finds lots of friends and is happy for the first time in his life. But the dark wizard Lord Voldemort, who killed Harry's parents, tries to regain his powers to

rule the world. It seems that Harry is the only one who can stop him.
Each book tells the story of a year at Hogwarts. In each year Harry has to face new problems and is constantly threatened by Lord Voldemort and his "gang". And he finds out that friends are the most important thing in the world.
If you think *Harry Potter* is another boring children's book, you are wrong! Each volume is exciting right through to the end. You'll meet dark creatures, find out about the wizard-world and you'll feel with Harry in his fights.
I'd recommend the books to anyone. They are much more exciting than the films.
I'm sure you'd love them, too.

1 What can you ask?

When people tell you about books, games or films, you often want to know more. Collect ideas for questions. Form questions like the ones below.

Books

What is the book about?
Is it easy to read?
...

(Computer) Games

Is it exciting?
What do you need to be able to play it?
...

Films

Who's in it?
What kind of film is it?
...

2 What would <u>you</u> recommend?

Think of a film, book or game which you either liked or didn't like at all. Give your own opinion by writing a short text. Say why you would/wouldn't recommend it. Use the questions you collected.

Test

1 Read this report from a school magazine. Fill in the correct forms of verbs, adjectives and connectives.

________ (read) is a waste of time!
I ________ (not like) reading. I think it is the ________ (boring) thing in the world.
Why should I read if I can ________ (see) the film?
Teachers and parents always say that reading is ________ (good) for children, because it ________ (develop) the imagination as well as the speaking and writing abilities.
I ________ (think) reading is just a waste of time.
Take "Harry Potter", for example. Many friends of ________ (me) read the first and second book.
Okay, they liked them, but it ________ (take) them several weeks to get through them, because of the many pages.
After they ________ (finish) the books, they ________ (have to) wait nearly a year for the third volume. When it finally came out, they ________ (forget) what ________ (happen) in volume two.
And when we ________ (go) to the cinema to watch the first "Harry Potter" film, they were really disappointed. "The book is much ________ (good)", they ________ (say).
And "Harry is so different from what I imagined him to be like when I ________ (read) the book!"
For those reasons I ________ (not read) books! I have plenty of time ________ (play) games on my computer while my friends are trying to get through all those pages.
Besides, for every good book there ________ (always/be) a film, so why bother reading?
In my opinion, teachers and parents should leave us kids alone!

You get 1 point for each correct answer. **Your points:** ________ /20

2 Translate the following sentences into English.

1. Ich ziehe deine Meinung seiner vor (= to prefer ... to).
2. Wenn ich jetzt nicht lese, habe ich nichts zu tun.
3. Wenn er mehr lesen würde, wäre er sicher besser in der Schule.
4. Wenn ich mehr gelesen hätte, wäre ich in der Schule besser gewesen.
5. Wenn ich reich wäre, würde ich den ganzen Tag lang (= all day long) lesen.

You get 1 point for each correct answer. **Your points:** ______ /5

3 Fill in the gaps with the correct form of the irregular verbs in brackets)

1. Once upon a time there ______ (be) a little girl who ______ (have) a dog. They often ______ (go) for walks in the fields together.
2. The dog always ______ (catch) mice, because it ______ (think) it ______ (be) a cat.
3. But one day one of the mice ______ (bite) the dog in its tail. “Hey, you ______ (hurt) me”, protested the dog. “I ______ (not do) anything to you!”, ______ (say) the mouse.
4. “I ______ (just hide) in your fur (= Fell) from that boy over there. Look, he ______ (throw) stones”, continued the clever mouse, who always ______ (know) how to get out of trouble.
5. The dog just ______ (shake) its head and ______ (leave).

You get 1 point for each correct answer. **Your points:** ______ /15

Your total points out of 40 points: ______

- More than 35? Very good.
- More than 27? Good.
- Less than 20? Have a look at the grammar and mediation pages again. You CAN do better.